The CFO Philosophy

To a child with an MBA, the world looks like KPIs

The CFO Philosophy

To a child with an MBA, the world looks like KPIs

Jacob Henricson

BUSINESS
BOOKS

Winchester, UK
Washington, USA

JOHN HUNT PUBLISHING

First published by Business Books, 2020
Business Books is an imprint of John Hunt Publishing Ltd., No. 3 East St., Alresford,
Hampshire SO24 9EE, UK
office@jhpbooks.com
www.johnhuntpublishing.com

For distributor details and how to order please visit the 'Ordering' section on our website.

ISBN: 978 1 78904 381 5
978 1 78904 382 2 (ebook)
Library of Congress Control Number: 2019945026

A CIP catalogue record for this book is available from the British Library.

Design: Stuart Davies

UK: Printed and bound by CPI Group (UK) Ltd, Croydon, CR0 4YY
Printed in North America by CPI GPS partners

We operate a distinctive and ethical publishing philosophy in
all areas of our business, from our global network of authors to
production and worldwide distribution.

Contents

Introduction

It was a family business that had thrived for almost fifty years under its original founder. A man in a small village in the middle of nowhere had seen a need in the market and invented a radically new product. Keeping close to his customers *and* his business, he had built a small empire that now spanned the globe, but with its heart in the village where it all started. As he grew old and finally died, his legacy carried on for some years under the stewardship of his children. As they could not agree on the direction of the company, and none of them had any real passion for management, they sold the company to corporate investors.

The name stayed the same, as did the core products, but quickly things began to change. The investors brought on young, ex-McKinsey and BCG consultants as managers and started buying and incorporating competitors across the globe. Ten years later, I was brought in as a consultant. Stepping into the corporate headquarters, I felt right at home.

After fifteen years in Corporate, I knew the drill. I could cross off the usual suspects on the first meetings: a five-year strategy had been developed, an ERM-system implemented, a matrix organization had been constructed. IT, sourcing and Finance management were in the process of being standardized and centralized in order to lower costs. A Management Excellence program had been started where managers were trained in "leadership". New recruitment processes were being introduced where each candidate was tested in a "personality assessment" by a cadre of "HR specialists". Secretaries and admin staff were being replaced by "automation" and various software. At least that was the idea.

The headquarters, located in the capital, were stylish and had conference rooms with names that were so clever that the

Leadership Team (née Management Team) must have spent at least a couple of off-site-retreats to come up with them. Suit-clad gentlemen (and women) passed me quickly and silently on my way to the clever conference rooms without saying hello.

The initial presentation of the company also followed a familiar pattern: 2-3 slides to set the tone and establish the company as a) having an interesting history (storytelling) and b) being "socially responsible" in some flavor (equality, sustainability or philanthropy). Then came the organizational chart and the "cost efficiency" program slides, followed by a recent re-organization. Everything looked smooth and was fully predictable.

As the project progressed, I started meeting with the original crew (I think of them as "the Locals"). The bulk of them had worked in the company for decades and still held on to their local, hillbilly dialects. They dressed in jeans and t-shirts and had a notable lack of respect for titles and fancy clothes. But they knew their business. They had never met someone who worked with IT Security before, but when asked, knew everything about how to secure their products, because they knew their products, and their customers and their technology. They had little patience for discussing compliance, project management or Sarbanes Oxley, but loved to talk about their products and their customers. They were also afraid.

The Suits were quick to talk about the lack of "execution" in the organization. They complained that the Locals were unorganized, did not have processes, did not have steering documents and – worst of all – did not Execute The Strategy that the Suits had spent many global business trips away from their families writing. In their opinion, the biggest problem of the organization was that the Strategy was not Executed. That, and the fact that the Locals did not know how to give a proper PowerPoint presentation.

The Locals were feeling the heat. There had been lay-offs and most of the Locals had no possibility for alternative careers in the small town where the heart of the company was located. Their mortgages and existence as they knew it depended on them being continuously employed at the company that they had already given the majority of their life to. They were afraid of losing their jobs but did not understand what the Suits wanted from them. So they started asking for more resources and pointing fingers at each other. And that is how I came in, and dozens like me. To do the work that the line organization was perfectly capable of doing, if they could apply some common sense and have a little trust in each other.

The Suits, on the whole, were indifferent to the suffering of the Locals. Sitting in the corporate headquarters, or in the airport lounges, they had little understanding of the plight of the Locals, their poor taste in clothes and utter lack of understanding of whose ass to kiss at corporate headquarters. Their knowledge of the actual business that the company did consisted of knowing all the numbers, coupled with the occasional "management-by-walking-around", i.e. putting on a hard hat and being escorted around the factory by one of the Locals. Sure, they met with customers occasionally, but usually with Suits on the customer side as well.

To control the Locals and get them to do "Strategy execution", elaborate organizational charts were set up with control functions. KPIs were introduced in a general meeting (over Skype), pushed out and followed up. New Senior Vice Presidents were recruited. A "project office" was set up with dogmatic processes to follow and PowerPoint template reports to be filled in. "Playbooks" and steering documents were written by consultants and pushed out to the Locals. A Senior Vice President for HR was recruited who introduced "talent management" and bell curve rankings. Controllers were brought in to make sure costs decreased by introducing elaborate approval processes (you could no longer buy a pen without "grandfather approval"). SAP was implemented, and IT was centralized – no more "local IT". Monthly reports were required from all parts of the business but never read by the person they were intended for. Incentive programs were introduced to make sure that people who exceeded their KPIs were rewarded with an extra bonus. People who learned to play the game advanced in the corporation, often at the expense of employees who kept their head down and tried to do the real work. All in all, it was a pretty dreary environment.

If you have never been in a workplace like this, you are lucky, and maybe this book is not for you. But what I have seen during fifteen years in corporate, variously as an employee, a manager and a consultant is that this is the direction most organizations of any size are headed. A special breed of managers is taking hold of corporations worldwide; the CFO's (a.k.a. controllers, MBA's, Change Agents and Innovation managers). Trained to believe that management is a skill in itself, they see no need to bother with in-depth knowledge of the subject matter that they are supposed to manage. Instead, they approach the job armed to the teeth with knowledge about Excel sheets and numbers. You can recognize them by the knowing smirk they display when they throw out the phrase "what gets measured gets done", as if it was said for the first time in the history of mankind. They are, what my surgeon friend called them; "the cold hands" of the business.

Of course they meet with opposition; old farm-hands who know their business and challenge the assumptions and pat solutions; owner-led businesses; investors with true understanding of the products and services. But generally, in the long run, the CFO way becomes the only way, because of two very important factors: 1) their general assumptions about the world (as I will try to show later in this book) are shared by most people, in a less extreme format, and 2) since the CFO's rarely work with the actual products, services or customers, they have almost unlimited time to play the politics at headquarters.

Slowly, one organization at a time, the CFO's are taking over the world, pressing their numbers-based view on everything. And as the public sector is always under pressure to reform, the CFO Philosophy has found its way into government authorities and the public sector as well. But some things cannot be measured reliably in numbers. Responsibility, initiative, loyalty, happiness are some metrics that are difficult to get right. And there is no room for ethics in Excel sheets.

Breaking up with corporate

I grew up in Arjeplog, Lapland, Sweden. Just below the Arctic Circle. One of my first jobs was planting trees. Where I grew up that was a common occupation for young people during the summer breaks from school. The work was led by an old lumberjack who was too physically worn out from a life of hard work to do much else than lead us youngsters and keep us from harming the forest or ourselves. The work paid 23 öre (about 3 cents) per tree planted and the quality criteria were unambiguous: the plants should be placed firmly into the soil with a distance between them of around three meters. It was hard work, physically, and the mosquitos and rain made it mentally exhausting as well, but the camaraderie when we stopped for lunch by a fire or got into our minibus for the hour-long drive home in the evenings made it better. And the pay of course. As a 15-year-old, I could plant 4000 trees in a day and it took me many years before I got up to an equivalent salary later in life. It was one of the few occasions in my life where my work has been measurable, simple and the results almost completely within my control. The harder I worked, the more money I got.

The "management" exercised by the old lumberjack was quite simple. He did not speak much. When he spoke, we listened. He knew the forest well and would always take time to show us things we came across during our work day such as bear-tracks or eagles. He reviewed our work by putting a stick in the ground, extending a piece of string and counting how many plants we had put within the radius of the string. If it was too densely planted, we got in trouble. Or, rather, he would just casually mention how many plants he had found, and if he was unhappy, it would show in his eyes. Getting "the look" was worse than any punishment he could have thought up, because we trusted him, liked him and did not want to disappoint him. We rarely cheated or worked sloppily, because it was important that we did not. Erik, our boss, was a real leader. And planting trees was a real job.

Unfortunately, after several summers spent in weeks of sub-arctic rain I came to a regrettable conclusion: I was going to get a job that did not require me to work outdoors. Some years later, having studied political science and becoming what F Scott Fitzgerald called "that most limited of all specialists, the 'well-rounded man'"[1], I stumbled onto a career in crisis and risk management. As it happens, I got my first job when someone dialed the wrong number and got me instead of whoever they wished to talk to. With my winning smile and outgoing character, spiced up with some self-deprecating humor, I soon made it into a corporate career. After some years as a consultant, I landed a job with a Fortune-500 company in telecommunications. I was quickly promoted to the role of Chief Information Security Officer and became globally responsible for the firm's information security, with a small team of professionals to help me. In 2009 I made one of my first very discouraging discoveries about C-level life: nothing I did or thought really seemed to matter. It was hard enough to get the people who were my direct reports to do what I wanted, but to get a global organization of 120,000 individuals in 180 countries to work in the same direction was mostly impossible. A clever salesperson at IBM who I met at the time summed up the situation for me: "So you have accountability but no mandate?" It was really depressing.

After realizing that I was mostly a figurehead with unlimited liability, there seemed to be just a few general options open to me: I could either accept the situation and do my best to cling on to the position by becoming Really Good at Politics, or I could strive to increase my mandate in different ways. Being young, naive and still wanting to change the world, I chose the latter. I liaised with the new CIO, who was also responsible for Sourcing, Real Estate, Compliance and a bunch of other areas. The guy's budget was slightly smaller than Sweden's total military expenditure.

I figured that getting into his leadership team I would be able to learn from the Big Boys and Girls how to steer the ship. I was – by far – the least experienced member of the team where several of the others had moved between senior leadership roles for 10-20 years with thousands of employees under their leadership. But, as one of my new colleagues leaned over and whispered to me during one of our first management team meetings: "It doesn't get smarter the higher up you go."

Actually, that is only partially true, the people in the leadership team that I joined were very smart. But the reality of business on that level was that most of them ran between meetings 8-10 hours a day and not a lot of reflection was done. Things that could reasonably only be solved by someone with good judgement and true insight were bounced around for months or even years in committees because no one at higher levels knew enough about the subject matter to dare risk a decision that had very unknown consequences, or if they made a decision it was often unclear exactly what it meant to the people below. Instead, most of my colleagues spent the majority of their time in committees and follow-up meetings. In the meantime, a lot of thinking was done by external management consultants.

A few weeks into my new job, I was beset by the KPI people for the first time. KPIs, or Key Performance Indicators, are measurements that purport to show progress towards set targets. The name indicates that they should be used as indicators, but in reality, they often become targets in themselves. The unspoken assumption seems to be that if all the KPIs are met, then the goals are met automatically, as a consequence. Around me, there was a cadre of bureaucrats that seemed to have only one goal in life: All The Excel Cells Must Be Filled In. At first, I was intrigued but gradually my frustration grew. I refused KPIs I did not believe in but had to do battle regularly with the KPI police and colleagues who were so used to KPI-steering that anything that did not have a KPI attached to it seemed suspicious.

In the world where I spent most of my waking hours, nothing was for certain. I took over an IT-security dashboard from my predecessor that after years of investments and hard work now showed green on most indicators. The problem was that it did not really mean anything. The fact that the dashboard was now green had absolutely no correlation with the risk of being hacked the very next day. The key is the metrics: which metrics show you that your risk is low? Despite billions invested in consultants and tools for risk management across the world, no one can truly answer that question. The reason is that most of cybersecurity moves in the world of "unknown unknowns" as Donald Rumsfeld so aptly described it. We have no idea what we do not know, but it can come and bite us any second.

As I fought the metrics and KPI people I started feeling that corporate was a strange place. The focus on KPIs and metrics made the work dull and unfulfilling, as well as difficult to accomplish. Instead of focusing on what I thought I was supposed to do; keep the organization safe from cyberattacks, I spent more and more of my time doing other things, such as writing reports, asking for permissions in exotic processes and systems, or going to training or coordination meetings. I felt like I had several managers. Even if I agreed with my boss on what to do and how to do it, I still had to have separate approvals from Finance, HR, Communications and quite possibly The Kraken. More often than not, our goals conflicted. And since everyone was being measured and incentivized on their own metrics, there was little room for mutual understanding and compromise. Common sense was in short supply, and it seemed to me that the systems we used to try to make the organization better actually created more problems than they solved. At least, they consumed an enormous amount of energy and time.

I experienced what could almost be described as a culture shock. The constant controlling, quantification and oversimplification of complex issues that went on around me was like the buzz of a new city to me, like the first time I visited New Delhi, Beijing or New York. Just like inhabitants of a foreign city, the indigenous people were so used to the sounds and smells that they did not even notice them anymore. The bureaucratic KPI-type management was so prevalent that no one noticed it or challenged the assumptions that lay underneath it. At the same time, the bosses were asking for innovation, talent, responsibility, sustainability, empowerment and engagement. All things contrary to what I felt would come out of a KPI-management philosophy. As I started questioning specifics, I realized that I was not getting through to the central issues. I was winning small victories – at the cost of being considered a trouble-maker – but not changing the flow of the main battle. I needed to understand the underlying assumptions and history of management better.

I started asking around: what are the principles, or the philosophy, of the management systems we have today? Where do they come from? How do we know that they work? What is the alternative? Most of the time, people did not even understand my question, or referred me to *Good to Great*, *Seven Habits of Highly Effective People* or similar light-weight reading. I realized I needed to try and figure it out for myself, but I had large gaps in my training. I had no real financial competence, schooled as I was in Political Science, so I set out to catch up on what I had – possibly – missed by not getting an MBA.

The – short – history of management

Where do the MBAs come from? I have tried to find books about organizational leadership dating back to pre-20th century, but mostly failed. The few examples I have found are focused on the domain in itself (i.e. a book about managing mines is 99% about the actual mine work, with some general advice on management thrown in for good measure). Leadership was an element of the job in the field in which you were active. A Master Smith was in essence a smith, with some management responsibilities. A Mine Master knew everything about how to extract metals from stone, and also had supervisory functions.[2] In that context there simply was not enough resources, or even a need, to maintain a large group of people who did not know the trade and whose only job was "to lead". The master was not a "manager" in the modern sense. Of course, "managers" with no particular skillset have always existed – the well-rounded men – in the form of aristocrats, clergy and administrators, but they were far fewer than today and had very different contexts for their work, as I will get back to later.

For the longest time, general management was the domain of military generals and the Catholic Church. For thousands of years, Chinese, Greeks, Romans and many others have written about war and how to wage it successfully. Sun Tzu's *The Art of War*, Machiavelli's *The Prince* are both staples, together with many others, for military leaders and have been for millennia. These books, and many others, have become classics for how they are written. They have told each new cadre of officers and politicians something useful about strategy and how to lead big organizations in uncertain circumstances. Granted, their success was counted in human lives and territorial gains, but there is still much to be learned for the power-hungry careerist.

The Catholic Church also knows a thing or two about management. In its lifetime it has survived a staggering list of challenges. For example: The Roman Empire. Attila the Hun. The

Moors. The Protestants sacking and looting the Sistine chapel. Napoleon. The third Reich. Some threats have come from within, like the time there were three popes (the Western Schism), or the "Cadaver Synod", when Pope Stephen VI dug up his predecessor Pope Formosus and accused his rotting corpse of perjury.[3]

And yet, the Roman Catholic Church survives. In management literature, the church is often held up, together with the military, as bad examples of old school, hierarchical structures that are outdated and should be replaced with "flat organizations" or "Digitalization". As it happens, almost exactly the opposite is true for the church. Many are fooled by the formal organization with popes, cardinals, priests and monks in a seemingly strict hierarchy, but that first glance belies the true wielding of power within the organization. Historically, one of the basic principles of the church has been *subsidiarity*. In a very basic interpretation, that means that decisions should be taken at the lowest level possible.[4] That way, the Pope has always had limited powers to affect what has taken place in different parts of the church, and they have had to adapt and fend for themselves.

What has perhaps tied the Roman Catholics together for millennia is not the formal organization elements or the authority of the pope, but a strong belief, coupled with the comfort that routines, social work and a community offers. As historian Eamon Duffy put it, writing about the first beginnings of the Church: "*In the melting-pot of empire, Christianity alone seemed to offer a single overarching intellectual and moral frame of reference, a simple code conveyed in vivid stories by which men and women could live. The parables of Jesus struck home where the arguments of the philosophers faltered.*"[5]

It was not until the industrial revolution that we started seeing "Management" as a profession in itself. Why? Well for one thing, we were entering uncharted territories. With the advance of the railroad, telegraphy and engines, more people could be brought to work together on the same endeavors than any time before in history. Humanity needed new knowledge to cope with the scale of things. In previous times, when encountering problems, we turned to religion. But religion did not have any answers on how to organize large-scale manufacturing or logistics. But maybe Science did?

In 1911, Fredrik Winslow Taylor published *The Principles of Scientific Management* and thus more or less established the idea of management as a Science, and management as a profession in itself. [6] The book was instrumental in establishing Harvard Business School, McKinsey and other management institutions and seems to have been the point where the idea that "management" was a unique task in the organization of production became widely accepted. Management, all of a sudden, became a discipline and skill in and of itself. For the first time, you could choose a career in "management", switching between industries and subject areas with great nimbleness, only bringing along your "management skills" and a genuine desire to be the boss.

"Scientific management" was an idea whose time had come. It came at a time when Science was conquering all fields. Naturally, it was time to bring it to bear on management as well. But is management really a science?

Chapter 1

Ideas have Consequences

In the late 90s a group of people calling themselves the Animal Liberation Front wreaked havoc in the quiet university city of Umeå in northern Sweden. Fed up with just talking about animal rights, they took action. Between 1994 and 1998, over 200 ideologically motivated attacks were reported to the police.[7] The activists, who were lumped together in media under the headline of "militant vegans", took inspiration from Peter Singer and others' ideas about animal rights. Taking the ideas of philosophers to the extreme they threatened and intimidated scientists, torched meat transports and released minks from farms into nature (with disastrous consequences for the local ecology). The counter-reaction from society was strong and they were labeled as terrorists in the media. This was before 9/11 and after Rote Armé-Fraktion, so the threshold for being called terrorist was a lot lower. Also, it was in a part of Sweden that traditionally was calm, even by the standards of a country that fought its last war during Napoleonic times. Naturally, feelings ran high.

Against the recommendation of everyone I knew, I had started studying Political Science at the university in Umeå at the time that this forgotten rebellion was taking place. The Master of Political Science degree that I was aiming for was jokingly also called "Master of extended newspaper reading" by the students and was sure to lead to financial ruin and a hellishly boring life in public administration. I blame my interest in the topic on a teacher I had when I was a foreign exchange student in Kansas in 1994, Mr. Overman. Before I took his classes on sociology and American history, I wanted to be an engineer.

During my time in Umeå, the local student union decided

to organize a debate with the Animal Liberation Front activists. The student union invited one of the most well-known and well-spoken activists, who accepted immediately, but had problems finding someone who would oppose him. Nobody seemed to want to sit opposite this extremely intelligent, angry and eloquent young man. Finally, the university chaplain was asked. In an American university this might have been a powerful person with high social status, but in secular Sweden the chaplain was a nice, meek and soft-spoken man with a beard. Our expectations were that he would be run over by a steam roller in the debate, but he seemed calm and content, nonetheless, so the debate went ahead.

In front of a small crowd of students, most of whom sympathized with the Animal Liberation Front, the debate began. The animal rights advocate delivered an eloquent and fiery speech, denouncing animal cruelty and laying out the text in rational defense of violence as a means for political change. The cause was more important than the means. It was fascinating, and it seemed like he had won the debate before the chaplain even opened his mouth. We all expected the chaplain to respond from a non-violence perspective, but he did not. When his turn came to speak he simply stated that their vantage points differed: "You think that animals are equal to humans in worth, but in my belief that is not the case. The Bible claims that humans were created in God's image, and therefore we are more valuable than animals. That means that we can use animals for food and experiments, if it benefits humankind. It does not mean we should be cruel to them, that we can agree upon, but as long as we disagree on the basic assumptions, we will never agree on anything of importance in this debate." The effect was disarming. The animal rights activist leaned back in his chair and thought about it for a few seconds and then agreed with the chaplain. Thereafter followed a pleasant conversation about history, philosophy and other things, which ended in a strong feeling of mutual respect between the debaters. None of them changed their fundamental view.

The debate was a disaster. No nerve, no heated arguments, and the moderator struggled to find an angle that would lead to some crowd-pleasing attacks, but to no avail. The tense and oppositional mood in the room died with the sober analysis of the chaplain. For me it was an a-ha! moment that I often think about. It brought home to me the conclusion that many disagreements can only be solved by going to the root of beliefs, and that the beliefs lead to choices and actions in real life. Without understanding the belief system that operates under the surface, it is often hard to understand the actions of people with opposing views to your own. Without knowing how they view the world, their actions may seem like trying to connect the dots without knowing the order in which to do it. For example: trying to understand American politics by reading Swedish newspapers is almost impossible, the only logical conclusion for a Swede, coming from a radically different set of views on mainly the social issues, is that Americans who vote for Republicans are clinically insane. Even the right-wing parties in Sweden would probably, at least until recently, vote for the Democratic candidate in the US.

Tolstoy described this beautifully in Anna Karenina. One of the main characters, Levin, is involved in a discussion at a society dinner in Moscow.

Levin had often noticed in arguments among the most intelligent people that after expending enormous efforts and an immense number of logical subtleties and words, the disputants at last became conscious of the fact that the thing they had been at such pains to prove to one another had long ago, from the very beginning of the controversy, been known to them, but that they liked different things and were disinclined to mention what they liked lest it should be attacked. He had experienced the fact that sometimes in the middle of a discussion one understands what it is that one's opponent likes, and suddenly likes it oneself and immediately agrees with him, when all proofs become superfluous and unnecessary.[8]

As I made my career in corporate, I came across ideas that were as rock solid as the chaplain's belief in the Bible. The general assumption seemed to be that everything could be measured in numbers, that things could always be done faster or more efficiently (typically 5% "Year Over Year"), that control was better than trust, and that – generally – setting and measuring targets was the only real model for steering. When I started asking people around me what the "ideology" of top management was in my company, most of them looked at me with bafflement and shook their heads. No ideology, just increase shareholder value. Be careful not to become theoretical. But by reading management literature and discussing it with other managers, I have nonetheless come to the conclusion that corporate is highly ideological, and that there is nothing unique about corporates view of the world. "Corporate philosophy" reflects much of political philosophy in the world, with one major difference: the dissenting views are suppressed in the board rooms based on the idea that corporations are not ideological. "We are not here to talk, we are here to make money." But as others have pointed out before me, there is always an underlying ideology in what we do. Ok, turning on the coffee machine cannot be done in many ways and ideology makes little difference, but as complexity and scale grows, ideology matters more. If you think crime starts with a poor childhood, you suggest placing resources into family homes for kids with problems, into education, into youth programs etc. If you believe that crimes should be punished severely and that punishments translate into reduced criminality, you suggest putting resources on police and jails. When the connection between cause and effect is unclear, ideology plays a larger role.

The same is true for corporate politics. A lot of the internal infighting and politics that I have seen in corporations has been more about the right way to do things, than personal differences. For example: should we spend more on R&D to harvest profits in the future, or should we spend the money on a better service organization to keep the customers we have today happy so they will buy more? All organizations grapple with issues like that, and my experience is that the larger the organization is, the more interests come into play. In a small organization, it is possible to sit down in a room and agree on the best way forward, but in a large organization the stakeholders are too many, and the issues too complex, to be able to decide on all issues by sitting down and talking about them.

As I continued my intellectual exploration I discovered, to my surprise, that a university education in Political Science came in very handy at headquarters. Turns out the CFOs have their own philosophy, but it took me a long time to figure out what it was. The pedigree is not pure, it mixes things like Scientism and an extremely pessimistic view of human motivation. It is based on the shared conviction that management is a science, that can be researched just like any other area and that "natural laws" can be found that – when implemented – produce the desired outcomes. It is an idea that is perpetuated by consultants, CFOs and their alma maters – the business schools – all around the world.

So yes, there is certainly a widespread idea that management is a science. But is it really? Before we can answer that question, we must break it down into its components and look at what "science" really is. Doing that without being theoretical is a challenge, but bear with me.

18

"Evidence-based"

What is science? As I am writing this, the debate and feelings run high in the wake of Brexit and the Trump election. There is a strong self-proclaimed pro-science camp, who are talking about a "post-truth-society" and anti-science sentiments spreading in the world, which should be combatted. Today the enemy is the pro-Brexit voter or the "deplorables", as some of the Trump voters call themselves after Hillary Clinton's use of the term. That is today, but the phenomenon is not new. In another time, religions were the enemies of "science", and vice versa.

I am university-trained in Sweden, Denmark and have studied in Spain and the US. I have debated with creationists, religious fundamentalists and communists, but I have never, until recently, seriously reflected on what "science" is, and what it is not. I have carried along a notion that could benevolently be called "Popperian", which is what I think most people intuitively think of as science. Science, in that interpretation, is a method. Often referred to as "the scientific method", its premise builds on setting hypothesizes and testing them, rejecting the ideas that are disproven and holding on to the ones that are confirmed by evidence and are peer-reviewed. A more popular way of expressing that is "evidence-based", that is, evidence supports your hypothesis. The more the better.

Karl Popper created the distinction between "science" and "pseudo-science" by defining the scientific method. Only by postulating a hypothesis that could somehow be proven false, or falsified, could science call itself science. Creating a hypothesis that could not be falsified was not science, but "pseudo-science". His example was to compare Einstein's theory of relativity, which could be disproven at a solar eclipse, and Freud's theories on the human mind, which could be fitted to any evidence, and thus could not be refuted. "Evidence-based" in this context means something that has not been falsified – yet. The totally opposite policy would be something like gut feeling. Gut feeling is rarely invoked as an argument for anything important today, because it denotes subjectivity, and we hate subjectivity. As we strive to avoid (ideological) subjectivity, we turn to science for objectivity. Evidence-based science.

But the way "Evidence-based" is used today seems to me like "it says so in the Bible" did when I was a foreign exchange student in Kansas. Saying that something is evidence-based and, preferably, touted by someone with an e-mail address from Harvard, MIT, or some other Ivy-league institution will silence the critics the same way as referring to The Word of Yahweh does in religious communities.

Associated with that belief is another belief: that Universities produce science, through academics, who also enjoy some of the highest levels of trust when we – the people – tell pollsters who we believe in. From the view that universities produce science comes the notion that everybody who works in a university is a scientist, and with the credibility Science has, that means that we typically attach more weight to their opinions than – say – a typical CEO who has an opinion about something. But of course, not everybody who gets their salary from a university does science. Science is not a profession, it is a way of trying to discover nature's secrets, that happens to often take place in universities. Or put in another way, the likelihood that someone who works in a university does science is probably higher than average, but it is not a 1-to-1 relation. A lot of junk science comes out of peer-reviews as well.

"Politicians" as a group typically rate low, which is probably why politicians do their best to anchor their views on science. In any public debate, you will always find politicians leaning on academics who give a "scientific" view of what is going to happen if we chose or do not chose a policy. Academics lend their credibility to politicians, albeit with some hesitation. As philosopher John Gray has put it: "Today, when politics is unconvincing even as entertainment, science has taken on the role of mankind's deliverer."9

"Science" and "evidence-based" has also spilled over into politics in more active forms. The term "Evidence-Based Medicine" was coined in 1992 as "the conscientious, explicit and judicious use of current best evidence in making decisions about the care of individual patients.". The concept was extended to other fields of care as "Evidence-based practice", and later to other fields, such as Management and Policy. Under the Blair government in the UK, a report called Modernizing Government stated that Government "must produce policies that really deal with problems, that are forward-looking and shaped by evidence rather than a response to short-term pressures; that tackle causes not symptoms." And who could argue with that?

The problem with "evidence-based" and human affairs is that it is often unclear what the cause is and what the effect is. In other words, what does the "evidence" prove? When it comes to medicine, the cause and effect is sometimes very clear: a person in pain who gets a pain reliever has less pain. Using a control group, side effects can then be studied and that will generate evidence for further treatment. Looking at policy, it is not so clear cut. Carefully designed and thought-out public housing areas become epicenters for crime and poverty. The war on drugs and terrorism leads to more drugs and terrorism, instead of the opposite. Building new freeways to relieve congestion leads to more congestion. But not always.

"Evidence-based" is just the latest iteration of an old dream to make the world less subjective and more rational. The Technocracy Movement that originated in the US in the 1920s aimed to replace business people and politicians with scientists and engineers that had the technical expertise to manage politics. Before that, various thinkers since at least the French revolution have proposed models where society is led by scientists, in a "rational" fashion. The problem is that when scientists enter politics they become indistinguishable from politicians. The reason is that politics will never be objective to any large degree, and the variables are too many to find the crisp and clear causality that launched the natural sciences into a spot of public veneration.

It is impossible to find a "scientific" answer to questions such as what is a reasonable age for retirement? Should we allow capital punishments? Abortions? What, if any, is the limit to how much resources we should spend to give a cancer patient two more months to live? Sure, arguments can be backed up by scientific evidence (often referred to as "facts"), but ultimately all those questions, and many, many more, need to be decided on feelings, principles, ethics and other things that cannot be captured neatly in a randomized control trial. Being an academic or scientist does not give you any further qualifications for making those decisions. Beware of people that start sentences with the statement "Scientific studies have shown."

The magic of science has been to reveal to us things that our senses cannot tell us. When dropping an apple on the ground, our senses tell us very clearly that there is up and there is down, and the apple is going down. We cannot see that the earth is round or that gravity pulls us to the planet we stand on. But with careful observation, using our senses, deductions, curiosity, creativity and experiments, we have been able to figure out things that have had an amazing effect on our life and quality of life. We cannot see bacteria (without aiding our senses), but using deduction and observation, Semmelweis found that they existed and thought of how to prevent them from spreading in maternity wards. We cannot see antibiotics, or the impact they have on bacteria, but Fleming discovered their effects, which led to the greatest increase in life expectancy in the history of mankind. Science helps us to methodically move beyond what we intuitively, based on our sensory perceptions, think is how the world works.

Moving into modern physics, chemistry, medicine and

astronomy, even aiding our senses is not enough. We cannot even imagine what a quark looks like or how an electron behaves in relation to a neutron. The world we can see and experience has not prepared us for such knowledge – our minds tend to translate everything into things we can understand and are used to. But that is not good enough for science. If we limited ourselves to interpreting the world through our own senses and familiar mental images of how things relate to each other, we would not have been able to make important discoveries and build things such as computers, atomic energy or modern medicine. Instead we use mathematics. The numbers reveal the world to us in a way that we do not fully need to comprehend, we just need to understand the math behind it. And we know that we understand it because we can produce repeatable results. Put in another way: in science, common sense is often wrong, but the numbers never lie.

The Scientific Method: observe – find patterns – predict – control (all expressed, preferably, in numbers) is translated freely into all areas of society with little regard to whether it is suitable for the context or not. We know that the first step, "observe", can be skipped if you study the same object again. For example, after you have dropped two hundred different rocks with the same result in speed and impact, then you can probably skip that step next time. All rocks – in that context – display the same properties. Intention is not important, nor feelings. It does not matter if the rock wants to drop, or if someone hurt its feelings by calling it a calcified lump of mud, it will still drop according to the laws of physics. The laws that apply to one rock apply to all rocks, with some known variations such as weight, size, shape and density. The same goes for most inorganic objects, which is why we can have general "laws" of physics and chemistry. But anything outside of the realm of inorganic things are subject to things that are hard to measure and generalize about. It is not impossible, but the context matters. A lot.

But all science is merely interesting if there are no practical applications. The telegraph was technologically mature for decades before it found widespread practical use with the railroad. Today we have graphene, which for years has been touted as the next revolutionary material, but so far no one has found a killer application for it. An interesting discovery to be sure, but it has not had any practical consequences yet. The greatest triumph of science has been that it improved our material quality of life and life expectancy tremendously. Having delivered something like heaven on earth, science naturally took the place of religion in many people's mind. The improvements came mainly from the natural sciences, so why would we not use that methodology for other areas as well? Gradually, the scientific view of the world moved from the natural to the human domain, spawning sciences such as sociology, informatics and psychology. It was only a matter of time before the ideas were applied to management as well. And there it finds fertile grounds in the heart of the modern man, Stephen.

Stephen – The Modern Man

Stephen is a modern man. He works in an office, managing a team of people and doing clever things with PowerPoint slides for his superiors, including – but not limited to – slide transfer animations. He studied political science at a semi-reputable university and has since complemented that education with an MBA at the local business school. He has three kids, a gigantic mortgage, hates Trump and loves his wife. He only goes to church for weddings, but always feels that the minister should focus less on the religious things and more on getting the wedding over with. His wife works full time, otherwise they would never be able to afford their mortgage. They both worry about the environment and do what they can to save the world. Mainly, their efforts to save the world consist in changing their patterns of consumption and berating family and friends who do not. They eat meat only every third meal, buy organic food, recycle their waste and one of their cars is a Tesla. The other is a diesel-driven SUV but hey, the kids need to go to soccer practice. Stephen reads Malcolm Gladwell and watches Youtube-clips by Jordan Peterson (behind his wife's back). He dreams about owning a motorcycle but wants to wait until the kids get older. He promotes women in the workplace and regularly gives money to a charity. Stephen is a stand-up guy. A perfect specimen for the 21st century.

Stephen has regular discussions about humanity with his friend, Robert. They have both heard of – but never read – Richard Dawkins and Nietzsche, but share their sentiment that God is dead, and that mankind has moved on to a higher state of being. We now have Science and know that previous generations were wrong in how they viewed the world. Stephen believes that his ancestors were victims of the church and its demagogues, but when they discovered the scientific method, they broke loose from the chains of ignorance. Robert disagrees with him slightly and believes that humanity as a whole has evolved in a consistent pattern, starting with tribes, moving through religion and monarchy and finally ending up in the best of worlds, the one we inhabit now. The Scientific World.

As Hayek wrote in *The Counter-Revolution of Science: Studies on the Abuse of Reason* in 1956:

> The discussions of every age are filled with the issues on which its leading schools of thought differ. But the general intellectual atmosphere of the time is always determined by the views on which the opposing schools agree. They become the unspoken presuppositions of all thought, and common and unquestioningly accepted foundations on which all discussion proceeds. When we no longer share these implicit assumptions of ages long past, it is comparatively easy to recognize them. But it is different with regard to the ideas

underlying the thought of more recent times. Here we are frequently not yet aware of the common features which the opposing systems of thought shared, ideas which for that very reason often have crept in almost unnoticed and have achieved their dominance without serious examination.[10]

Even if Stephen and Robert disagree on some topics, they share so many assumptions that taking opposing sides does not mean that they fundamentally disagree. For example: Stephen thinks the European Union is great. He believes it brings Europeans closer together and makes life better for all the citizens. His prime argument *for* the EU is the inner market, where products and services can move freely. Robert, on the other hand, thinks that the bureaucratic machinery in Brussels has far exceeded what is reasonable and thinks that the EU budget should be decreased, mainly the portion that his own country pays with his tax money. What they both tacitly agree on, without realizing it, is that if the EU was dismantled overnight, some other international institution should take over its role in the world, because international institutions make the world better. Stephen and Robert both carry a classical, liberal view of international politics (as do most Europeans), where interconnectivity through free trade and exchanges on cultural and political levels prevents war and make the world a better place. These are the people who are drunk on Stephen Pinker's and Hans Rosling's rosy interpretations of how the world is striding along to globalization utopia. When Stephen and Robert come across someone from the typical *realist* school of international relations, such as Henry Kissinger, or John Bolton, they are dumbfounded, because that person has a fundamentally different view of how the world works.

Another tacit assumption that both Stephen and Robert share is that Science can answer all questions, given enough time and resources. Plastics in the oceans, antibiotics wearing off, environmental problems are just a peer-reviewed study away from being solved. When discussing climate change, they often refer to the statement that "most scientists agree", or even give a number of how many have signed the UN accord on climate change. All in all, Stephen and Robert have a pretty stringent and strong view of the world and how it works. They need it, their existence relies on it.

Imagine if science cannot solve the problem of antibiotics losing their effect and we were once again brought back to a world where infections killed 53% of the population and the life expectancy again became 40 years as it was before the industrial revolution. Imagine if we ran out of oil and coal and science could not replace it, bringing us back to manual harvesting of food sources and no elevators in sky-scrapers. Pollution would quickly become the least of our problems. There are many other candidates on the list, but these two areas are the most scary ones to contemplate, because if we ran out of antibiotics or oil without replacement, we would very quickly descend into a medieval world, with many, many casualties on the way.

I think this is the reason why I have met with such strong reactions when I have dared to question the omnipotence and omniscience of Science (with a capital S). In Stephen's world, I am not questioning a method (even though it is called "the Scientific Method"), I am questioning their core beliefs about themselves and the world. And just like Christians and the Bible, or Muslims and the Koran, that is where it starts to hurt. You can argue many things on the way, but if you challenge someone's core belief, you are putting their back against the wall. Everyone has core beliefs, and they usually come from the context they were raised in. Some are rebels, and break out of that fold, but the majority of us just plod along down the path that our parents, first girlfriend or schoolteachers set us on.

When I had just turned 18, I traveled to McPherson, Kansas, to spend a year as a foreign exchange student in an American high school. As it turned out, my host family were devout Christians of a Baptist denomination, so my first introduction to my peers in Kansas was through the youth group of the church. At first, I was skeptical about the idea of meeting friends through the church. Not because I had any staunch opposition to religion, it was just that my view of the church in Sweden was that the only kids who went to church were nerds and social outcasts. I was very positively surprised that there were many cool kids and good-looking girls in "my" church group. After a couple of weeks, we went to church camp and did most of the stuff that kids in Sweden would do at camp (except drinking and having sex). I was thoroughly enjoying myself with my new friends and euphoric with the realization that kids are the same all around the world. Any misgivings I had had about fitting in in my new school vanished among the laughter and bantering with my new friends. Then came the final evening of camp. A group of us boys, all testosterone- and puberty drunk eighteen-year-olds, stopped what we were doing and stared in awe at the night sky. I had never seen such a sky before. The Milky Way was visible as clearly as if it had been drawn on a chalkboard. It was – in the original sense of the word – awesome. Then one of the boys found some words and exclaimed: "Can you believe that there are people who see this and still believe that we evolved from monkeys?" I turned around, ready to get in on the joke and start spinning it along, when I saw his face. He was dead serious. So were all the other boys as they quietly nodded their assent. This was my first brush with Creationists. I felt the ground shifting underneath my feet and got very, very homesick.

What I had experienced was that friends, my age, funny, witty, cool, intelligent and interested in the same things as me at that age (girls and sports) held a completely different belief in a core issue than I did. Previously, I had only heard Creationists mentioned in passing as left-overs from a pre-Galileo time, when people were dumber than we are today. I thought that they were gun-wielding troglodytes with the common decency not to intermingle with normal people. But these guys were just like me! I became obsessed with understanding *why* they would believe such a preposterous thing. I took the discussion to Sunday school. What I quickly discovered was that they not only knew all my arguments, they had arguments against them. When I asked them how they could believe such nonsense, they immediately turned the question around on me: how did I know that evolution was real? Sadly, my arguments were shallow. I had never, ever questioned evolution, which meant that I had not really looked into the proofs for it. I understood the general idea, but I had a hard time backing it up with evidence and it all came back to the same arguments that they were using: it sounds reasonable, and I was never taught any alternative by my parents or in school. Ok, it might be that I am less well informed than my peers, but years of playing the Devil's advocate at parties and dinners has convinced me that I am not alone. I have amused myself (to the consternation of my wife and friends) by defending bull-fighting, the NRA, Trump and the death sentence. Usually I find that people are so unused to meeting someone who disagrees with their view of the world that they cannot formulate their own arguments.1[1]

Now, many years later, I am still certain that evolution has led us to where we are, and I still do not think that Creationism should be taught as a viable alternative in school. I have read up on evolution and know my Dawkins well enough to counter all the arguments of fundamentalists on "the other side". But the episode taught me (I believe) to be humble in the face of radically different core beliefs than my own. Explaining why people believe in Creationism or voted for Brexit with the analysis that they are "stupid" is stupid in itself.

There are areas where religion excels. For many people religion offers the only key to mental health. I have met many people across the world who have been pulled out of their darkest despair by belief in something supernatural. Yet even that statement is challenged by people who hate religion. The worst haters of religion are the ones who have had it crammed down their throat by parents, priests or the society they grew up in. I have – fortunately for me – not had that experience, so I cannot muster any particular aversion for religion as such, just for the fundamentalists who are not content to have their own road to salvation but must force everyone else to follow the same path that they do. But those are not unique for religions.

My point is not to say that "Religion" is better than "Science", just that neither of them are omnipotent, and they should not be treated as adversaries. In extension, because science is not omnipotent, we should automatically look at the *quality* of science that comes our way. This is particularly true in the field of social sciences, and for the purpose of this book, the management "sciences" as taught at the business schools around the world. Just because it is peer-reviewed does not mean it has any value, it might even be harmful. But still it is used without afterthought in most organizations.

Leadership: art or science?

So having explored management's relation to science, I want to come back to what Management really is. As explained before, "management" as a concept was invented along with scientific management, but the challenges management faces are far older. If you are the boss, regardless of which age you live in, you will have to deal with – at least – the following challenges, which are all older than language:

- Managing ambition
- Dealing with conflict
- Dealing with sloth, conspiracy and treason
- Time pressure and conflicting demands
- Uncertainty and stress

- Ethics and morals
- Death and disease

The CFO Philosophy belief in finding a "model" or "tool" that works for every possible situation has generated a bunch of quasi-scientific nonsense that may be an inspiration, but ultimately does not save any time or effort and may even cause damage by oversimplifying things that should be treated with afterthought and respect.

Rocket surgery leadership

Applying for my first position – at a government agency in Sweden – I was subjected to the "Myers-Briggs Type Indicator-test", which was supposed to identify my "psychological preferences" in how I "perceive the world around [me] and make decisions."[12] The test, which is one of the best-known personality tests in the world, mimics psychology and purports to be scientific, but has zero predictive value or validity. Later, working at a small consulting firm, I was sent to mandatory management training and received distilled wisdom of management such as "7 Habits of Highly Effective People" and "The Situational Leadership® Model". When I became a manager and was expected to rank people. I was introduced to "Talent Management" and "Forced Ranking". Being a member of a leadership team, I was expected to cooperate in "creating" and disseminating "values" across the organization. Doing all those things is supposed to ensure that organizations only get the "right people" inside their perimeters, and that they are managed scientifically along the way, to create the best results with minimum waste along the way.

Business schools teach how to be a good manager and Harvard Business Review publishes empirical studies recurrently. Google, true to its credo to organize the world's information, started what it called Project Oxygen in 2008 to try and nail down what separates a good manager from a poor one. Three years later, after some serious number-crunching sessions, Google's team came to the conclusion that there were eight (not ten, nor is the number six) habits that highly effective managers exercised:

1. Be a good coach
2. Empower your team and don't micro-manage
3. Express interest in employees' success and well-being
4. Be productive and results-oriented
5. Be a good communicator and listen to your team
6. Help your employees with career development
7. Have a clear vision and strategy for the team
8. Have key technical skills, so you can help advise the team[13]

Not exactly rocket science. And that is the point. Rocket science, as seen in the Apollo project, is a very precise science. You can calculate and test things that – even though they are very, very complicated – can be repeated with the same results every time. Humans, on the other hand, are, in the words of Michel de Montaigne, "[A] marvellous vain, fickle, and unstable subject, and on whom it is very hard to form any certain and uniform judgment."[14] As anyone who has several children knows, results may vary. Just when you thought you had figured out how to parent, you get a second child that responds very differently from the first one to your upbringing. Is it because you are different, or the child is different? And is that difference biological or does it depend on the environment? The debate rages on, but nobody really knows for sure (though many claim to).

The problem is the same when it comes to good leadership: it is elusive. The philosopher turned Management Consultant and then turned philosopher again, Matthew Stewart, expressed his view on a good manager in his book *The Management Myth*:

A good manager is someone with a facility for analysis and an even greater talent for synthesis; someone who has an eye both for the details and for the one big thing that really matters; someone who is able to reflect on facts in a disinterested way, who is always dissatisfied with pat answers and the conventional wisdom, and who therefore takes a certain pleasure in knowledge itself; someone with a wide knowledge of the world and an even better knowledge of the way people work; someone who knows how to treat people with respect; someone with honesty, integrity, trustworthiness, and the other things that make up character; someone, in short, who understands oneself and the world around us well enough to know how to make it better.[15]

Stewart has here expressed Google's 8-point list, before it was made, but in a vastly more eloquent and even poetic way. But even Stewart has an unspoken assumption that is often found when talking about good management or leadership: that it is benign. A good leader wants to make the world and the people he or she leads better. However, that is not necessarily true. It depends on how you define what a "good leader" is. Does it mean someone who is well liked by staff and other people, or someone who reaches results, or both? If they achieve results, is it better to reach short-term results or long-term results? Some of the most influential leaders in history are remembered as horrible people that were dangerous to be close to or in the way of: Stalin, Hitler, Pol Pot and Mao, among others. Notwithstanding their cruelty and terror, without a doubt they "delivered results", as the current management speak goes.

Jack Welch, himself an experienced leader, expressed his view in a matrix: you can have high results or low results, and you can do it according to the values of the organization or by not adhering to those values. In his opinion, and mine, we often promote the people that achieve results, regardless of whether they adhere to values such as respect, integrity and honesty, that are nominally valued in most organizations. Meanwhile, the HR function tells managers/leaders that their most important job is to motivate people, to promote equality and to be role models. That is of course only partially true. The most important thing, in most organizations, is to achieve results. Everything else is secondary. How secondary depends on the pressure in the organization. Very high pressure will make people do very strange things to keep their jobs and reach their goals.

How you achieve results with your team, regardless of what results are defined as in your organization, is more like football than engineering: everyone can learn the rules, but few excel. Managing people and small groups is more art than science. Everybody understands that you use a canvas and paintbrush to make a painting, but that does not make you the next Da Vinci. You need inspiration, training, experience, luck, aptitude and a host of other things to succeed.

If you can see their eyes it is personal

True leadership is direct and personal. It is here and now. It is organic, with warts and all. It is the leadership of heroes and villains, of Thermopylae and Jonestown. Of Odysseus and Hernan Cortéz. Of selfless sacrifice and cruel destruction. It is the sort of leadership that can make people perform miracles against all odds or break all their inhibitions and gut feelings to afflict terrible cruelty on each other. This leadership is as old as time and as fleeting as smoke. We know it when we see it, but we are still not sure how it is done. It is unaffected by science and technology: there exists no gadget or theory that will improve leadership skills that did not exist thousands of years ago. It is difficult – or impossible – to control as it depends so much on individual capabilities, preferences and dynamics between those people.

True leadership is being captain of a sailing ship. The captain steers his ship with a crew through sunshine and storms. The power is seldom undivided in the captain's hands and mutiny is always an option, but the responsibility for success and survival rests firmly with the captain. In a crisis situation, the crew will turn to the captain for guidance. The captain can lock himself in his cabin but cannot hide from the crew and the fate of his ship, exposed as they are, together.[16]

But there is another kind of leadership that is symbolical, structural and organized. It is lever-pulling, programming and engineering. It is broadcasting orders and messages and developing "strategies". It is "culture" and organizational charts. It is centralization versus decentralization. It is the leadership of the King, the Pope, the President of the United States or the CEO of a Fortune 500-company, but it is also the head of the government agency, the school system or the hospital. It is the projection of power through signals, such as clothing, protocol, edicts, laws and state-of-the-union addresses. It seems to start when groups are too large to control by the leader personally looking each member in the eyes, or direct communication is impossible for geographical or technical reasons. It is often called bureaucracy. It is also as old as civilization, but in this domain, technology has had a huge influence.

Where is the borderline between a captain and a king? Of course, there is a certain degree of overlap. A king is a captain for his court, but a king to the rest of his realm. It seems that the fault line lies where it is no longer possible to exert influence directly. Robin Dunbar, a professor of evolutionary psychology, has given name to Dunbar's number. Dunbar's number is a suggested cognitive limit of how many individuals we can sustain stable relationships with. Dunbar identified the concept initially when doing studies on apes and has suggested that the number is 150 for humans. Even though I think the evidence is a bit sketchy, I can relate to the concept of small groups having another kind of relationship than a large group. In Arjeplog, where I grew up, there lived only about 1600 souls. That was small enough that everyone was connected to everyone else through at least two "nodes": my friend's father was also my soccer trainer. The cashier in the store was grandmother of one of the kids I played with. My classmate's mother was also a patient of my father. Those connections lead to full social integration. The social control, but also support, becomes very different from living and working in a big city as I do now. A well-known phenomenon of living in a small city is that you cannot hide. Your strong sides and your weak sides are on glorious display, as opposed to big cities where people can choose which sides of themselves they want to display in public (or on social media), and there is a clear distinction between "public" and "private". In a small city, private and public are almost completely overlapping.

The same goes for organizations. It is difficult to hide weakness from your closest co-workers. In a small company, at least outside of the management consulting industry, the managers are close to their subordinates. They may say one thing consciously and signal something completely different subconsciously. The Vice President enters the building with her head hung low, goes straight into her office without greeting anyone in the team. After half an hour in seclusion, she emerges with a forced smile and talks about how great things are going. The signals are there for anyone paying attention: things are not going well and she is doing her best to hide it. Leadership consists of both these kinds of signals, but in large organizations, the unconscious symbols can largely be filtered out. A CEO or Executive Vice President with a Communications department can choose the time and manner with which he or she speaks to the staff and tailor the performance. Much like a king of the past, ceremony can sensor out the unconscious signals. That is probably the reason why most employees are awash in "information" but still complain that they are uninformed about the strategic direction of the company.

Real leadership is about presence. Physical presence. Being physically present and dealing with the people you lead eye-to-eye allows people to truly get to know each other. In contrast to tailored messages broadcast from the CEO office, a Captain shows him or herself in all their glory or despair to their subordinates. They broadcast intentional as well as unintentional messages. A frown here, a slap on the back there may make all the difference in a project or stressful situation.

Leadership of this kind is older than time and often idolized, like many other pre-modern things, but the truth is that it could be – and still is – both beautiful and brutal. It is harder to fire your coworkers that you meet every day than it is to fire 800 employees in another country by closing a factory.

Not much has changed, not in our way of leading and not in our knowledge about how to lead. The 7-, 8- and 10-point lists that Google, Harvard and others churn out by the thousands may serve as great inspiration, but they will never be an actionable guide in the sense that a recipe for baking bread is. There are simply too many variables when interactions between humans take place. And when the number of persons to lead and coordinate increases, complexity increases.

There have always been religious, political and military leaders who have commanded vast hordes of people, but not in the sense we see today. Without means of communication, local leaders became single authorities for most of the time for their teams. Decentralization was not one of several options, it was a given. High level power struggles existed, but the day to day business was between the leader and the people he was supposed to lead, with a commander somewhere far in the distance with very little idea of what actually went on with his subordinates. Few leaders were completely autocratic, and they have always had to relate to other powers than themselves, but essentially, leadership was conducted between a team and its leader, with limited day-to-day involvement from the outside.

Reinventing Excellence with the Why

Steve Jobs was one of a kind. His legacy is an inspiration for people all around the world, but how did he become so successful? Books have been written about him and his leadership style and genius. Young people around the world study his deeds the way that the ancient romans once studied the lives of noble Grecians and Romans in Plutarch's books. But while the ancients treated these stories as inspirations, something to aspire to, our age instinctively looks for patterns, rules and generalizations to repeat.

It is not impossible to study – for example – the success of Apple, Google or Microsoft and make some general observations about what led to that success. Furthermore, there is nothing to stop you from constructing "rules" or "recipes" for repeating their success. On the contrary, many books have been sold on this premise, most notably *Good to Great* and *Built to Last* but in recent times also quasi-religious, new-age management books like *Reinventing Organizations* and anything by Simon Sinek. But there is a huge difference which should be evident to anyone who thinks and observes the world: knowing the "rules" of management does not generally lead to predictable results. And that undermines the claims of being "scientific". A theory that is proven wrong half of the time without anyone knowing why is not science, it is astrology and Tarot cards. As inspiration, those books are great, but taken literally – like the laws of nature – they become dangerous. It is like pressing a square peg in a round hole: if you do not press, nothing will happen, but when you press hard, something will break. What will break depends on the material of the peg, the hole and the box you are trying to fit it into, but something will break. The same is true for organizations. Trying to reach impossible targets by oversimplifying the world will lead to cutting corners, burning out staff, cooking books or any number of negative consequences that we see on an almost daily basis in media. Skipping the problem definition before setting targets and KPIs will lead to unintended consequences. Using "balanced scorecards", "Activity Based Costing" or having a "Chief Culture Officer" will not save you, it may worsen the problem because it is yet another way of treating unique problems with pat methods without reflection.

Many others have identified this problem before me, but I could not find anyone who had tried to explain *why* management is performed in this mechanical way. Most of my inspirations merely identified the problem and then moved on with a shrug of their shoulders, or pointed fingers to a specific group; bureaucrats, middle-managers, psychopaths. The easiest explanation to why managers keep trying to control people using naive "Science" is that they are all idiots. But I was raised in a small community and have a good-natured trusting view of the world. I think there are reasons that can be both identified and understood.

Invisible patterns of humanity

Like Stephen, the modern man, many of us carry a notion that we have evolved mentally to where we are today. In a non-descript sense, we must be better in some way than the ancient Egyptians or Incas. But there is no proof that this is the case. Ok, some things have changed, especially in the last few generations, where we have become taller, fatter and live longer, but there is no evidence that our minds are different from our ancestors who founded Jericho some 12.000 years ago.

Over the eons, the way we think and what we expect from the world seems fairly stable. There seems to be a certain "human nature" that is hard to correctly capture. Decades of post-modern philosophy and debates essentially claim that this is not true and that all our notions of the world are constructed (and can thus be deconstructed). Of course, like many other ideas, this one is not completely without merit. If it were, it would have disappeared already. We can see that our attitude to many things has changed over the centuries. The Greeks, for example, kept slaves and said very condescending things about women. That would not be possible in todays (western) culture. In their time, it was not okay to criticize the emperor the way media run after world leaders these days. Some things change, undeniably. Even (or especially) between generations things change. Conservative parents have reactionary kids. But in the longer perspective, much remains the same.

Today we are proud to have democracy, but three-four generations into the modern version of democracy (there have been many others before), there is a worrying tendency for power to become hereditary again. The Clinton, Bush and Kennedy families have subscribed to important positions in American politics for decades, including presidencies. The Gandhi family has influenced Indian politics for decades. The current prime minister of Canada, Justin Trudeau, is the son of a former prime minister of Canada, Pierre Trudeau. Similar "coincidences" can be seen in most democratic systems around the globe, leading to the question: do we have a human need to trust a family in power, and not just an individual? Are democracies en route to becoming what that monarchies have always been – hereditary power transfers within elite families?

Other institutions that seem to survive whatever we throw at them: marriage (sometimes religious, sometimes not), harvest celebrations, dancing, alcohol consumption, prostitution, holiday celebrations, funeral ceremonies, families, war and of course organized religion itself, albeit in various forms. Some of those things we, as humans, have tried very hard to get rid of at times when they have been out of favor, but they always come back in a very similar form. It seems that we have a basic human need that is perhaps not rational, but needs to be satisfied nonetheless.

Nassim Nicholas Taleb, statistician, trader and thinker has championed a lot of different concepts and ideas within uncertainty and randomness. One of them is the Lindy effect. It was formulated in 1964 by Albert Goldman, but Taleb has incorporated it into his view of the world in the books *The Black Swan* and *Antifragile*. The Lindy effect states that contrary to living things, inorganic things like ideas and technology, are more likely to survive in the future, the longer they have survived up until now. Taleb builds on the Lindy effect for the following definition: *For the perishable, every additional day in its life translates into a shorter additional life expectancy. For the nonperishable, every additional day may imply a longer life expectancy.* He exemplifies with himself:

> *Tonight I will be meeting friends in a restaurant (tavernas have existed for at least twenty-five centuries). I will be walking there wearing shoes hardly different from those worn fifty-three hundred years ago by the mummified man discovered in a glacier in the Austrian Alps. At the restaurant, I will be using silverware, a Mesopotamian technology, which qualifies as a "killer application" given what it allows me to do to the leg of lamb, such as tear it apart while sparing my fingers from burns. I will be drinking wine, a liquid that has been in use for at least six millennia. The wine will be poured into glasses, an innovation claimed by my Lebanese compatriots to come from their Phoenician ancestors, and if you disagree about the source, we can say that glass objects have been sold by them as trinkets for at least twenty-nine hundred years. After the main course, I will have a somewhat younger technology, artisanal cheese, paying higher prices for those that have not changed in their preparation for several centuries.*[17]

This idea is alien to the way most of us are raised. We have reaped the benefits of technology that seems almost like science fiction and thus have a technology optimism which is staggering.[18] When we talk about new times, we (willfully?) forget that most of the challenges we face in life, humanity has faced before.

The Lindy effect is another indication that we have the same needs over time. The only difference today is that we have more technical tools than ever before, above all communication.

Looking back at past history, we can perhaps find the patterns that will reappear in management, but also the evolution that has led us to the management philosophy we have today.

Chapter 2

The CFO Philosophy

Technocrat - the origins of the species

Anno Domini 1576. At the end of a long and adventurous life, Girolamo Cardano published his autobiography. In it, he marveled at the technological wonders of his lifetime: the compass, the musket, the discovery of the New World and the printing press were changing the world while he was living in it. The world grew bigger and smaller at the same time, and the first information revolution was at hand. All of a sudden written information became available to the masses. Prior to the printing press, few people owned books. A monastery with a large collection had 500 books. Sorbonne had around 2000, but in the 16th century, an estimated 150 to 200 million volumes were printed.[19] An explosion of information gave way to other advances in society.

Cardano himself had an interesting life. He became an influential mathematician and made invaluable contributions to the theories of uncertainty and chance that were just beginning to evolve. As a newborn his wet-nurse, like many others, died from the plague and he grew up in a society that was marked by the loss of a third of its population. The world he grew up in was breathing out after the plague and all of a sudden there were plenty of resources available because the population was reduced considerably. Since then, the population growth has steadily gone upwards, with an exponential growth during the last 150 years. Ever increasing population, along with technological advances such as gun powder, telecommunications and mass transportation led to people organizing in ever greater endeavors. As a result of gunpowder being used in wars, the castle became outdated as a defense. In the 16th century, building of forts became such an expensive and complicated business that rulers started to organize work centrally, with prescriptions and inspectors.[20] Mining and smiting also came under the control of the nation states as the states were consolidated and needed ever more resources to wage war on each other.

During that period, the main source of energy was wood. Wood was used for heating, construction, mineral enrichment, cooking and pretty much every other application possible. As the world population increased and the technological progresses demanded more energy, prices of wood increased. During the 16th century prices increased six-fold.[21] Coupled with the so called "little ice age", a period of unusual cold in Europe between the 16th to 19th centuries, wood became a scarce resource. The research has borrowed the German word "Holznot" (wood shortage) to describe the situation.[22] The increase in price continued until coal started being used as a substitute. Coal could generate more energy than wood, and new applications and enrichments of coal were invented. Steam machines were invented in the late 17th century and gradually became widespread. With the invention of James Watts' steam engine in 1781 and the high-pressure engine invented by Richard Trevithick in 1797-1799, steam engines finally became efficient and compact enough to be used for powering trains. This – and other inventions – unleashed the industrial revolution, which has been continuing on the same exponential tangent since then.

The industrial revolution has brought material welfare unlike any previously seen in history. It has also brought us the technology to enable large scale control of organizations: instant communication. The famous parallel that it took five months for the world to find out that Columbus had landed in America, but it took just a few seconds to see that people had landed on the moon holds true for leadership as well: a CEO today, unlike a king or general of the past, can more or less instantly gauge his/ her organizations status by calling someone or – even better –

just look at a dashboard. As late as the time of the Napoleonic wars, it could take days for the Russian emperor Alexander to find out whether he had won or lost a battle in his own country. Today, most of that knowledge is instant. And that has had consequences.

Welcome to the Machine Ensemble, how may I serve you?

As railroad tracks were being laid across England in the early 1820s, there was still only a vague idea of how to utilize them in the best way. Or rather, the idea was to use them as an extension of existing modes of transport. The tracks were thought of as roads or rivers: anyone could traffic them in any way they saw fit, as long as they did not endanger anyone else (too much). So the first tracks were owned by the – often private – financiers that built them, but there was no monopoly on using them. Anyone could put anything on the tracks and drive it as fast as they liked. That included horses and private steam-powered trams. Surprisingly, it took planners, engineers and politicians a few years to realize that this was untenable. Accidents were common, but above all the traffic was congested by the slowest machine on the tracks.[23] Regulation was changed to give the owners of the tracks monopoly on utilizing the tracks. With no unregulated traffic on the rails, trains could drive faster, but that increased the danger of collisions. Lookouts were employed to look for meeting trains, but if it was foggy, or dark, it was sometimes hard to spot other trains before it was too late. Then someone realized that a previous invention was exactly what was needed: the telegraph. The telegraph had been around for decades, but seemingly found no practical use. As the railway extended its reach and traffic, the telegraph signaling system matched its needs. With the telegraph, the railroad company could plan the trips in advance and keep check on the progress from a distance through reports from stations. In essence, control of operations then moved from the train driver to a central headquarters which reduced the role of the driver to merely obeying orders in real time.

Columbus was the captain of his ship. What he did and who he was mattered. With the advent of telegraphy and railroads, along with other inventions such as standardized time[24], standardized production and systematic division of labor, the role of the "Columbuses" of the train world were reduced to being mere human parts of a machine. Wolfgang Schievelbusch, author of several books on the railway and its impact on the pre-modern world, has called this a Machine Ensemble. He writes: "The machine ensemble, consisting of wheel and rail, railroad and carriage, expands into a unified railway system, which appears as one great machine covering the land."

In the Machine Ensemble, who drives the train holds virtually no importance, a development we can see carried to its full conclusion today with Google and Tesla's self-driving cars. The personality, thoughts and leadership of the individual driver is almost irrelevant to the role and importance of the task they are expected to perform. The only importance of personality, culture and skills of the operator is negative – if it interferes with his or her work. The system is built around a set of tasks designed to be performed using a "least-common-denominator" approach to quality: the bar is set low enough that someone with minimal training can perform the work. McDonalds is a typical modern-day example of this, where the employees repeat mandatory phrases and perform standardized tasks in a mechanical fashion. The odd smile is appreciated by the customer but generally has low or no impact on profitability. Poor body hygiene, on the other hand, might. Thus, focus is not on excellence, but on upholding minimum acceptable standards. It is ok if no one is great, as long as no one is terrible. We go to McDonalds, knowing well that we will not get a first-class experience, but because we will get more or less the same experience (at a cheap prize) anywhere in the world.

In the machine ensemble, control is key. Fredrick Winslow Taylor, the father of "Scientific Management", realized this. His idea of defining targets and basing compensation on how they were reached was nothing radically new, the idea of incentive-based pay had been around as long as money, but the way he framed the principles were new. In his work The Principles of Scientific Management, he proposed the following:

"In the past, the man has been first, in the future, the system must come first".[25]

That is, in the past, who did the job was more important than what they did, but with new technology and knowledge, it was now possible to reverse that relationship. The worker becomes a tool for the machine ensemble, not the other way around. In the pre-industrial world, the artisans were unique. If ten 15th century gunsmiths made a gun each you would get ten completely different guns. Same function, but different caliber, parts and look. No inter-compatibility and thus no scalability, and total dependency on a master gunsmith or special parts if you needed repairs or changes. The drawback of this system is of course scale. How can you guarantee that different elements of an organization are moving in the same general direction? And how do you ensure that quality and delivery is sufficiently professional if all the workers are their own masters? How do you boost productivity and efficiency if everyone decides methods and working times by themselves? How do you negotiate the salary of a person that cannot be replaced? By defining some basic standards, such as caliber of the bullets, the guns may look different, but can still share the same pool of ammunition. By standardizing the parts repairs become simpler and cheaper, and the dependency on the person who built the gun in the first place is eliminated. Instead of having a person in particular doing it, anyone can do it.

Taylor's ideas, and those of his disciples, were hugely influential on the times they lived in. Science, and the scientific method, had great impact on people's lives, and the idea that it could be applied to humans and organizations in a systematic fashion opened up brand new opportunities. Taylor's book became the basis of the first curriculum of the newly founded Harvard Business School[26], which for decades delivered its top talent to McKinsey corporation and still is the top leadership institution in the world. Henry Gantt, disciple of Taylor and inventor of the Gantt chart, inspired Lenin and other revolutionaries at the onset of the Soviet Union, leading to the infamous five-year plans that are now mocked by those who remember them. The very idea of management consulting seems to have been born here. All of a sudden, young people with no real knowledge of the actual business at hand, could charge outrageous fees to advise someone senior to themselves who had spent whole careers in a field. The key was to transform management from something that came with the job to something that could be defined scientifically, and sold as "models". Looking at "management" from the side, actual knowledge of the field was not necessary. At least that was (and is) the idea.

The main idea behind Taylor's "science" still stands, more than a hundred years after it was defined. Taylor himself has become an object of mockery, and "modern" management gurus and consultants assure us that they have departed from his ideas into something more "modern" such as "culture", "innovation" or "digitalization", but the essence of what Taylor proposed is as alive today as it has ever been. In most organizations, it is championed by the most venerated of the Finance People, the CFO.

CFO, for those who have not yet come across one, stands for "Chief Financial Officer". They are typically trained at business schools with a focus on corporate accounting, but with interesting additional courses such as "Change Management", "Digital transformation", "Innovation" or similar subjects, whatever may be in vogue at the moment. In the last few decades it seems that the CFOs in many companies have had more and more responsibility thrust upon them and many have made it to the CEO position. In large companies, they often serve the role of "internal" CEO, regulating the budgets and targets of their peers while the CEO takes care of the customer meetings and inspirational speeches at Davos. The CFO is the ambassador of natural science methods in the management corridors. Their training makes them prefer "objectivity", preferably expressed in numbers, to subjectivity expressed in words, which they consider "soft". The numbers never lie. "What gets measured gets done".

Among them, over time, a mentality, or paradigm, has settled. It appeared first in the private sector and then gradually moved over to the public sector. I have come to think of it as the CFO philosophy. It borrows some fundamental ideas from natural sciences and those ideas then constitute the compass that guides managers when they look for direction. It rests on some ideas that are taken for granted – more or less – today, but that would have been considered radical in other times and ages.

CFO Assumption 1: The world is predictable

A true CFO believes that the world is perfectly rational and that everything can and should be generalized, standardized and measured. With some generalizations, everything can be compared to anything. "Benchmarking", "maturity models" and "GAP-analysis", where complex areas are reduced to a few defined variables which are in turn translated into targets (or Key Performance Indicators, KPIs) is the preferred way of working. Everything that can be put in an Excel sheet should be put into an Excel sheet. And since there are no epistemological limitations to what can be expressed in numbers, everything goes into the Excel sheets. Motivation, corporate social responsibility, ethics, customer loyalty are just some examples of what the Excel sheets have eaten in the last decades, even though there is plenty of evidence that this is not always a great idea. Even the future is defined in numbers, in the shape of "Risk Ratings" and "Strategies", where – typically – data about the past is extrapolated into the future without any consideration of the fact that most things that change the world, or even a business, are unpredicted. Along with this assumption comes the idea that you can control everything as well. If you cannot control it yet, it is just a matter of time and effort until you can.

According to the CFOs, measuring is equal to getting things done, and that not measuring things means that nothing gets done. This argument is sneakily prevalent in any discussion about New Public Management or KPIs: that the alternative to measuring and having targets is that nothing gets done. Without targets expressed in numbers, we enter "la-la-land" where everyone goes around their workplace with flowers in their hair without structure or deadlines and accomplish nothing. As one commenter expressed it on an article I wrote for LinkedIn Pulse:

> You have to have KPI's and metrics, and hold individuals, or yourself, accountable to them. I have never worked in an organization that did not have them. [...] If you do not have them, you will not have goals and objectives, and your business will flounder as a result. Lack of accountability will result in Camp Runamuck.

But there is more to the idea of rationality, targets and measuring than immediately meets the eye. Anyone who spends any time thinking about this stance realizes that many things are hard – if not impossible – to measure, but still this belief seems to flourish. In any organization, a person is never just a number. Let us take Paul as an example.

Paul is Paul, a whole person. Paul shows up late for work and rarely works the full 40-hour week. He is rude to customer VIPs and his salary is higher than that of his peers. He has a problem with authority and never, ever does his monthly report on time (or at all). He does not have a university education. He dresses shabbily. Paul does not sound like a great company man. On the other hand, Paul's self-taught knowledge of the software is unparalleled and the customers know this. They may not invite him out for lunch, but when there really is a problem, it is Paul they ask for and they are ready to pay for him. And Paul delivers where it counts. He will work 48 hours without sleep if needed. His peers also love him, despite his grumpy attitude. When one of them discovered a tumor, Paul took time off work to escort him to the hospital and stayed there until he could go home again. Among his peers, Paul is a legend, a true embodiment of the best of corporate spirit and values. But how do you convey that sort of complexity in a "talent management" system? How do you capture it in a "Meyers-Briggs test"? The answer is: "You don't." In those systems, Paul ends up as a non-flattering set of numbers that the closest manager will have to defend every time salary revision comes up. And that is the only way it can be, when all variables are reduced to numbers and control is centralized. Complexity gets lost and the executives make decisions based on aggregates of numbers, rather than on persons as persons. This approach is not completely without merits. It has worked great in revolutionizing "simple" work such as farming and factory production, but we are running out of simple work.

Especially where humans are concerned, rationality and predictability is the exception to the rule. Centuries of trying to turn "soft sciences" (such as sociology, psychology and behavioral science) to "hard sciences" by applying methods from natural sciences on humans have led to dismal effects. The scientific method is simple: by observing the world, we can find patterns and explain what happens. If we can explain it then we can predict it. If we can predict it we can control it. That method, as I wrote in a previous chapter, is applied with great effort to the world of humans. And sure, we are great at the first steps: observing (especially with the use of Big Data) and explaining. There are as many explanations for things as there are scientists, but few, if any, have made it to the next step: predicting. And if prediction is missing, then control becomes hard.

Douglas McGregor, known to anyone who has studied human relations, wrote in his book *The Human Side of Enterprise* in 1960, the following prediction:

Developments in physical science theory during the first half of the twentieth century have led to the creation of a new world. If anyone had been able to predict in 1900 what life in the United States would be like in 1960, he would have been regarded as a complete fool. Passenger travel 6 to 8 miles above the earth at 600 miles per hour, space vehicles circling the moon, radar, a nuclear-powered submarine traveling under the icecap at the North Pole, air conditioning, television, frozen foods, stereophonic reproduction of the music of world-renowned musicians in the home – these things and hundreds more were almost inconceivable sixty years ago. They would still be inconceivable were it not for developments in scientific theory and man's inventive genius in exploiting them. Although the parallel may seem unreasonable to some, we are today in a period when the development of theory within the social sciences will permit innovations which are at present inconceivable. Among these will be dramatic changes in the organization and management of economic enterprise.[27]

Looking back to 1960, when the book was written, we know now that we have another set of innovations that Douglas could not even imagine: iPhones, Spotify, the Internet, true mass transit of humans across the world, etc. etc. But what McGregor was really after, the advances in social sciences, is largely absent. We do not know much more about humans (outside the fields of biology and medicine) today than we did in the 1960s. We do not even know much more about humans today than we did 2000 years ago, when Greeks and Romans pinned their timeless stories and philosophies. For anyone who has read their books, it must be obvious that someone like Joseph Conrad, or Cervantes, or Hemingway knew much more about human affairs than any professors of sociology, history or economics do today. But this suggestion is deeply controversial to managers who have been through management trainings where they learn to use Meyers-Briggs tests, balanced scorecards or "Situation based leadership" as if they were saws, hammers or screwdrivers. They are even called "tools". However, unlike physical tools, they do not consistently create the same effects.

The social sciences even have a hard time replicating their own studies. The "replication crisis" was highlighted in 2015 when the respected scientific journal Nature published an article called "Over half of psychology studies fail reproducibility test".[28] In controlled form, attempts to reproduce results from 98 original papers failed in over half the cases. Similar tests have yielded similar results. If social sciences cannot even reproduce its own articles, there is serious reason to doubt that they have value for managers fighting in the everyday hustle of organizational life. That does not mean that social sciences are useless, as some government officials think, and that every resource should be invested in STEM (Science, Technology, Engineering and Mathematics) education. It just means that social sciences should have other methods, goals and expectations than STEM sciences. Social sciences are like culture: it is difficult to rationally prove their value to society, but there will always be a need for them. Why? Because we are humans, and we cannot always explain what we need or why we need it.

Interestingly enough, that does not mean that we have no

idea how groups of humans or individuals will act, but our knowledge is more based on "rules of thumb" than research and empirical facts. Many of those rules of thumb are manifested in proverbs and words of wisdom. Proverbs, like the classic books and stories, have come down to us like messages from another time. They have travelled through times of war and times of plenty and they have survived their time travel because they had something important to say to every age. They do not offer complete remedies for problems, but they remind us of things that are important, and time has sharpened their edge to the point that they are very easy to remember. Reading Don Quixote for the first time a few months ago, I was struck by the fact that even though the book was written more than 500 years ago in Spain, I am familiar with most of the proverbs that Sancho Panza uses to sprinkle his conversations with the Knight. In the words of the Knight of the Rueful Countenance himself: "I think, Sancho, there is no proverb that is not true, all being maxims drawn from experience itself, the mother of all the sciences..."

Assumption 2: Everything evolves to become better

The second assumption of the CFO Philosophy is that everything evolves to become better. There is always a better idea waiting around the corner. Every year Apple presents a new product which is a little better than the previous model. Each new car has improvements over the last model and companies that do not renew their product line at reasonably short intervals will soon find themselves out of business. "The experience curve", developed by the Boston Consulting Group in the mid-1960s, states that we can produce things cheaper and better every year.[29] Bruce Henderson, founder of BCG, expressed it as follows: "Costs characteristically decline by 20-30% in real terms each time accumulated experience doubles." The science of today "knows" more than the science of yesterday, according to the TED talkers. In short, everything gets better all the time, which is the extreme layman's version of Darwin's theory of evolution. At least, that is one of the basic assumptions of the CFO philosophy. Everything can be improved and made more efficient. Hospitals, factories, education, health care, ethics. We are just an innovation away from the cure for cancer. It is natural – it is inevitable – everything will be better in the future and everything new is better. There is an almost religious flavor to this belief: somewhere, beyond the Excel-sheets, Nirvana awaits. There is a perfect utopia somewhere, we just need to work harder to reach it. Much like the Christian belief in Heaven, we need to labor and suffer, but the perfect world awaits us. You will get pie(-charts) in the sky when you die.

This belief manifests itself in vocabulary such as "GAP-analyses", "Maturity Models" and the naming conventions that are embedded as naturally as e-mail in most organizations: "Next Generation X", "Product Y 2.0", even "Product Evolution". The idea stands in stark contrast to the experience of the majority of humans who have ever lived: things rarely change permanently. Instead of a clear path to utopia, human development to earlier generations came in waves, juxtapositions and balances: Yin and Yang, heaven and hell, Insha'Allah. Empires grew up and vanished, leaving only traces in the dirt of their former glory, but were in time replaced by others. In the rest of society, science-based utopianism during the 20th century led to the costliest experiments with human lives in the history of man: Stalinism, Maoism and National Socialism, and the appetite of current generations for large scale political experiments seems weak. Today the dominant ideology seems to be individualistic liberalism: give the individual as much choice as possible and try to get out of the way. Leave the hard decisions to bureaucrats. Few political parties, outside of the extreme left or right, today push utopian visions on their voters. For the time being at least, we the voters have become fed up with political visions of heaven. But in business it is another thing.

Business press is overflowing with visions of corporate utopia, whether they be called "Teal organisations", "Holocracy", "Lean" or any of the multitude of other systems and snack-size philosophies that promise to deliver the workplace into the CFOs Garden of Eden. We can always improve efficiency, technology, diversity and motivation a little more, and at the same time, with a newly discovered method. But what if we cannot?

On October 24, 2003, just past 4 p.m, the last Concorde flight landed in London. With it, the dream of supersonic passenger travel died, or at least went into hibernation. The Concorde project had been living on borrowed time since the last plane was built in 1979 and was abandoned after one of the Concorde's crashed in Paris in 2000, killing every soul on board. There have been other attempts to make supersonic passenger planes, but none have ultimately proved successful, for various reasons. Instead, the aircraft industry has made great strides in improving efficiency and lowering costs so that many more people now travel by airplane each year, than ever before. That is great, but those who lived during the moon landing in 1969 would probably have been surprised if they were told then that we have not come farther in 2019. A number of articles I have read claim that air travel is even slower today than 40 years ago, but I have found no conclusive statistic to prove it. Certainly, the feeling I have as a passenger is that it is getting slower and slower, mostly due to more rigorous safety checks.[30]

Why is air travel not faster? Because of ... reasons. Fuel economy, scheduling problems, increased air traffic and the willingness of passengers – or lack thereof – to pay for the extra cost. In other words, a combination of technical difficulties and people's preferences: we do not want it bad enough and it is hard to do. Post fact it seems like a logical conclusion that air travel speed does not continue to increase exponentially but looking into the future we seem to make the same mistake over and over again, because we have been brought up to believe that the future will always give us new and nice things that are better than the ones we have today. We have not discovered new major oil fields since the seventies? Elon Musk will fix that. Penicillin is rapidly losing its power to kill bacteria? The scientists will solve it. Africa is still poor after 50+ years of foreign aid? We just have to improve the methods of giving aid and put higher requirements on the aid organizations. Set targets (cure cancer/fix poverty/ end wars) break down into activities (appoint someone famous and set aside government funds/have billionaires donate their money/create new branches of the UN), measure progress and review. Everything will surely get better.

In this mood of reverence for the future, it is worthwhile to remember the words of Ovid, the Roman poet: "Iam seges est ubi Troia fuit" – Now are fields of corn where Troy once stood. In fact, Troy – once a great city – was so completely destroyed that it was believed that it had never existed until it was rediscovered in 1871 by the adventurer and general enthusiast Heinrich Schliemann. Great empires have risen and fallen for at least tens of thousands of years. There is no historical evidence that life and civilization follow a trajectory towards getting better and better all the time, because of our intellect and science. Such belief, as John Gray has pointed out, is more religious in nature than logical: "Most people today think they belong to a species that can be master of its destiny. This is faith, not science. We do not speak of a time when whales or gorillas will be masters of their destinies. Why then humans?"[31] There is nothing automatic or destined about progress. Any such belief is just that – a belief.

Still, for the CFO, progress is inevitable. Efficiency can always be improved 5-10%. Every year, targets are set based on this assumption across millions of organizations and on billions of professionals, usually without much afterthought. But there is of course a logical limit to efficiency and improvement as well. I brought up this point at a lecture I gave to students at

Chalmers University some time ago and used an example from my own life to illustrate. My father, who for most of his life worked as a medical doctor and head of a small care center in a rural area of northern Sweden, scoffed at political promises to shorten queues to operations or emergency care. He used to say that over time, it did not matter how many hospital beds or surgeons were available: the queues were always roughly the same length. I thought this was common knowledge and was surprised at the backlash I received from the students and even their (management) professors. They did not believe me. As one of them told me: "Are you trying to tell us that people abstain from seeking medical attention because there are queues?" And yes, that was exactly what I was trying to tell them! As the owner of a trampoline and father of three children I have repeatedly had to make the mental calculation when a wailing cry has risen from the garden: do I get in the car now to go to the emergency room or wait and see how bad it is? Knowing that the waiting time for a minor injury at the emergency rooms in Stockholm is 5+ hours (often in the company of sick, crying and vomiting kids who are also waiting) makes me quite reluctant to go. If nothing is visibly broken I wait at least an hour or two before reevaluating the decision. Had the waiting time in the emergency room been five minutes I would have been there at least three times as often. If the travel time was 2-3 days like it often was two generations ago in my hometown in Lapland, going to the emergency room had not been an option at all, unless the injuries were life threatening. People had to learn to take care of most injuries themselves.

My point is not that it is better to have long queues. Short queues do save lives and so does better health care in general. My point is just that it will affect costs. In the political discourse, there seems to be an almost universal assumption that health care, and other public goods can be made more efficient. That may be true, but unlike the private sector, where more customers mean more revenue, the public sector "customers" do not bring in more money, just cost.[32] More efficiency means higher costs. Lowering costs may actually come as a result of lowering efficiency, which sounds completely counter-intuitive to most people and is certainly very rarely proposed in political debates, but often quietly exercised.

The phenomenon described above is sometimes called Induced Demand and means that after supply increases, more of a good is consumed. It has become a controversial concept because it has been used as an argument against building new highways in the US. The line of reasoning is roughly similar to the above: cities like Los Angeles have spent lots of money building freeways and the traffic congestion just keeps getting worse. The argument is that as each individual makes a cost-benefit analysis of getting a car, building new roads leads to more people buying and using cars on a daily basis and thus congest the new roads. I think most people agree with this analysis, the controversy instead centers around whether to build new roads or not. In my view, the principle of Induced Demand should not be used to argue against new roads in itself. Instead, it should be used as a way to explain the effects of building new roads: more roads lead to more costs, but also to more travel, which might in itself have beneficial effects on society. It will not, necessarily, lead to a reduction in travel time for the individual, though. In a way the idea is similar to the Triple Constraint Triangle of project management. Any project manager with self-respect makes the steering group consider which tradeoffs they are prepared to make: they can choose to variously prioritize time, cost or quality, but not all of them, all of the time.

In the 1960s, economists William J Baumol and William G Bowen described the phenomenon that came to be known as Baumol's cost disease. It is the observation that, as efficiency grows in some sectors, wages increase also in the sectors that are not becoming more efficient. The example is particularly clear when comparing manufacturing industries with health care: over time robots and computers, combined with innovations in processes, have reduced the reliance on the human workforce in agriculture and industry. As fewer individuals are employed, but with a higher skillset, wages increase. In health care, processes and technology cannot replace humans to the same extent and efficiency increases has historically been much lower. Nonetheless, doctors, nurses and other health workers have an expectation of a certain level of salary, not least compared to their peers in the manufacturing industry. Mortgages are not cheaper if you work in health care. If a doctor's salary does not keep up with salaries in general, they may choose to exit the medical profession for something else that is better paid. The net effect over time is, according to Baumol's theory, that health care becomes relatively more expensive and constitutes a continually larger share of society's total costs. This goes not only for health care, but for any area where humans cannot be replaced by robots and automation.

In field after field we can see the same effect: improvements in efficiency or supply in a limited area lead to an increase in total cost. Yet the CFOs keep chasing efficiency in stovepipes: each "Head Of" in their organization gets assigned an efficiency improvement/cost cutting goal that is then "trickled down" in the whole organization, led by a central strategy. In public life, the expectation that evolution towards perfection through innovation or efficiency is always possible creates the same pressure for public agencies such as health care, law enforcement and school systems. The net effect is rarely that the whole improves, as intended, but rather that sub-optimization leads to unforeseen difficulties, such as cost increases, poor quality, infighting or other problems that nobody wants. The answer, always, is to increase measurements and bureaucratic control. But the assumption is wrong to begin with.

The Swedish language has a word that cannot be found in

English: "Lagom". It means: just enough. Not too much, not too little, just right. In Latin, there is an approximation: *ne quid nimis*. It means "nothing in excess" and has been attributed to the poet Horace. It is a simple sentiment, but underneath the simplicity lie vast oceans of obstacles. The most difficult expectation that underlies the CFO Philosophy is that everything can be better. Without realizing that we cannot develop, control and improve everything at once, there cannot be another way of managing. Imagine a CEO that tells the market that "we can't do better than we are doing at the moment". Or a politician that says that things are not perfect, but they are not really going to get any better. They will soon be replaced. Yet this realization is key to looking at other ways of leading. Again, it is the qualitative and often subjective assessment that is key. Some things can be improved, others cannot. Some things can be guaranteed, others we will never control, no matter how hard we try.

Assumption 3: Human motivation is created with a carrot or a stick

The third assumption that feeds the CFO philosophy is a pessimistic theory of human motivation which is charmingly simple: to get humans to perform, you either tempt them (the carrot) or threaten to punish them (the stick). Fredrik Hertzberg, a management scholar, has called this KITA-motivation. The best way to motivate someone is to give them a Kick In The Ass, but since that is illegal (in many countries) it has to be translated into economic incentives and threats. There has been lots of research into alternative methods and philosophies of motivation, maybe starting with the famous Hawthorne experiments performed in the 1920s by Elton Mayo and carried on by scholars such as Maslow and Herzberg himself, but the assumption is still as alive today as it has ever been. Much of what is taught at the different leadership trainings I have attended aims to teach managers to manipulate their subordinates. The tests, "situational based leadership", talent management et cetera exist with the primary purpose of getting people to do what their managers want them to do, whether they want to or not.

In a furious article called "Bad Management Theories Are Destroying Good Management Practices", Sumantra Ghoshal, a management academic himself, attacked Agency Theory and the effect it has had on corporations and other organizations the last thirty years. Agency theory, in its simplest form, means that someone (a principal) hires someone else (an agent) to do work, and that both are motivated primarily by self-interest. Since the principal (for example the Board of Directors) cannot count on the agent (for example the CEO) to do the work so it benefits the principal, a control/motivation structure needs to be set up to steer the agent in the right direction. There is a lot more theory behind this, presumably written by theoretically oriented scholars with too much time on their hands, but the general idea here is that people cannot be trusted to "do the right thing" without external stimuli. To me this is an advanced version of the KITA-theory, but by dressing it in scholarly clothes; fancy incentive programs and control mechanisms can be built which are based on "science". But as Ghoshal rightly points out, the idea that managers and staff cannot be trusted to behave ethically may be self-fulfilling, which is evident in the budget process of most companies.

At least in the places where I have worked, the budget process normally goes like this: The manager, we can call him Bob, asks his subordinates to make a budget estimate for the coming year. The naive subordinate, Bill (a first-time manager), returns with a figure that he believes is realistic. Then negotiation commences. Bob challenges Bill and tells him to take off 10% because "sandbagging" is not accepted. "Sandbagging" in management speak, is when someone requests more budget than they actually need, just in case. Bill fights to keep his budget but eventually has to accept a 5-10% reduction in a legitimate budget proposal and has to stretch his time and team to the breaking point all year to meet his aggressive targets. Next year, Bill adds 10% more than he thinks is needed even before negotiations start and Bob the Manager is thereby proven right: people cannot be trusted. They sandbag. If you are a salesperson this dynamic plays out exactly the same way, but in the opposite direction. Instead of reducing the line budget, the manager increases the "sales budget" to "stretch". One of the most successful sales people I know once told me that his key to success was getting his sales targets as low as possible.

There has been plenty of talk about "intrinsic motivation" since the concept was developed in the 1970s by Edward Deci[33], but little progress. Intrinsic motivation is the opposite of KITA-motivation. It is the motivation that comes from within, that inspires people to build things like Wikipedia, Linux and Apache servers without being asked to do it or paid for it. Intrinsic motivation defies the logic of Agency Theory: why would anyone spend unpaid and un-incentivized time and energy on doing anything at all (besides enriching themselves)? But as anyone who has coached a kids soccer team knows, there is some joy in the work itself. The "problem" with intrinsic motivation is that it will not let itself be generalized or quantified. That means it is invisible to the CFO. Sure, you can make a theory about it if you like, and put nice words in a PowerPoint presentation, but unlike KITA-factors, intrinsic motivation measures do not neatly translate into reality. You can make Bill work late by threatening to fire him, or by paying him overtime, but how do you make him motivated? In that relationship, the manager is the one who is motivated, not Bill.

How do you create intrinsic motivation? It depends. Some people are motivated by money. Others by social status, others by titles, others by noble purposes. But it varies, and thus cannot be put in Excel sheets and centralized. To the chagrin of the CFOs.

So if the CFOs cannot create intrinsic motivation, who can? Well not the managers of course, because the CFOs do not really trust them. Enter the HR department. HR stands for Human Resources, or Human Relations, but is often given other names. Where I have worked, HR has variably been referred to as "Heavy Resistance" or "Human Remains". Urban Dictionary refers to the HR department as "a non-value added component of many large companies. Human resources is a worthless division in a company that often has power beyond its members' level of intelligence. Human resources generally spends most of its time justifying its existence."[34]

I would not go that far, but I believe that the HR function is caught between conflicting missions. On the one hand they are tasked with attracting and retaining talent (in a sort of unexplained competition with the actual managers of the talent). On the other hand, they are management's prime tool for keeping wage erosion in check. On one hand they work to create motivation, on the other hand they enforce labor laws and negotiate on opposite sides of the table with labor unions, ostensibly the representatives of the workers.[35] In their struggle to be taken seriously, HR seems to have moved more and more into the domains of the CFOs. Employee satisfaction, talent, productivity, relative worth for the company are all measured and "managed" through numbers in IT systems. Like in everything, there are exemptions. Sometimes the head of HR is a wise person with a lot of experience who picks up "sticky problems" in the organization and sees to it that they are solved. But put too much pressure on the HR organization and they will become Motivation Gestapo, beating out intrinsic motivation, one manager at a time.

HR-people are also recruited directly from HR-schools that teach them Human Relations much like Management is taught at Management Schools. Again, the belief that Management can be taught in schools means that the HR departments of most organizations are populated by people who have no experience of managing people or business. They have their Excel sheets and tests, but can rarely answer complicated questions about human interactions. When I first became a manager, I took over a unit that had struggled for a while. The employees that I was supposed to lead were disillusioned to the point that they spent most of their time working against any new manager that took over, meaning they had had five different managers in two years. I was young and inexperienced, but sincerely wanted the team to regain their motivation and work well, or replace them with someone who could. I went to HR for help. The HR Business Partner, a 27-year-old on his first job, listened to me attentively and with compassion in his eyes. After I had emptied my heart he gave me a book called *Choosing Happiness* and recommended me to read it, reflect and come back later. I never came back.

During my time as a manager, I found that I increasingly needed approval to do the things that were expected of me as an employee and manager: travel, expenses, hirings, firings. Even evaluating the performance of my direct reports became the decision of a committee, led by HR, as part of the "talent management" program of the company. What this signaled, to me, was that the company paid me and my peers to do a job, but did not trust us to do it honestly. Often, when I looked into the history of things, there had been an episode where some employee had abused the trust put in them by behaving badly. But instead of just punishing that person, rules were set up to prevent the same thing from ever happening again. The expectation being that everyone is a suspect of repeating the wrong-doings of one person. Slowly, corporate life has moved away from presumed innocence to guilt-by-default.

The CFO priests and disciples

A philosophy without simple, practical applications will never be widely spread. The religions all know this. Rituals, routines, ceremonies and trinkets are all essential for the spread and attraction of religions. The CFOs understand this, or at least the management academics and consultants who have made a living off the CFO Philosophy for more than a century, starting with The Prophet himself, Frederick Winslow Taylor.

To a child with a hammer, the world looks like nails. To any problem, there is only one solution: whack it good (my living room tells that tale after having been handled by three kids). Likewise, to the CFO, there is one solution, or ritual, that fits any problem without further analysis:

1. Define (objectively) what needs to be done
2. Have someone do it
3. Monitor progress (quantitatively)
4. Reward or punish results
5. Evaluate and repeat

This simple model, The CFO Hammer, is ingenious in its simplicity. The trick is to define the desired results objectively – step one. If you can do that, then you do not need to know exactly how it is done or who does it. You can abstract the tasks and thus control them on a large scale. Like a child with a hammer, everything looks like nails to the CFO. It incorporates all the elements just mentioned: a rational world (1-3 and 4), dishonest workers that must be manipulated (4), and an assumption that everything can be made better through a project (5).

The CFO Hammer has been adopted to such an extent that we have a hard time imagining how to solve a problem without it. But just like many other things we have discussed so far, it works best when the work is simple and predictable and the variables are few and known. We have used the hammer so frequently that we seem to have forgotten that there are other management tools available.

Synthesis – The CFO Philosophy

Science has served us well. We are better off – materially – than ever before. But science applied to human interactions is elusive. What works great in some contexts does not work in others. Methods that are applied successfully in one area fail in another, even though the areas appear similar. That is not up for debate, it is a fact. Despite this, there is an almost religious belief in the power of the Scientific Method and in particular anything that is "evidence-based".

Economists are trained using natural scientific methods on a domain that includes humans. Over time, they have been quite successful, and a particular "CFO philosophy" has taken root and spreads slowly from area to area. Economists, speaking a language of their own, and very sure that the world works according to their designs, exercise control over companies from the CFO or CEO position. Market and corporate analysts employed by financial institutions, often with very little own experience of leading people, never mind complex business, dictate the fates of CEO careers in publicly owned companies, based on a few variables such as "working capital", "cash conversion rate" or "earnings per share". Management consultants from McKinsey, Boston Consulting Group and others prescribe the same method to all their clients, for outrageous sums of money. The CFO Philosophy makes it possible to have a legitimate-sounding strong opinion, without actually knowing the subject matter, and thus legitimizes a class of "professionals" who can alternate between executive positions in completely different fields, without ever truly knowing the organizations they are supposed to lead. All based on some very simple assumptions about the complexity of human interactions. I bet they have not read Tolstoy, or only read it for the romantic parts.

Anything that does not fit the CFO philosophy has the burden of evidence on its side. But the world itself, with all its complexity and mysteries, is refusing to cooperate. The more we try to shape the world and the humans in it to fit the CFO philosophy, the more unintended side effects we see, and the more boring the world becomes to us who live in it.

Chapter 3

More Haste, Less Speed

For the last few hundred years we have become better and better at organizing large groups of people to work together. The development has gone hand in hand with population growth and resource utilization: the more numerous we are, the better we need to use the resources we have at our disposal. As construction projects, mining, wars and cities grew larger and involved more people than before, we had to invent a new way of leading. The new leadership had as its focus to reduce dependence on individuals, and instead create a system that would work, regardless of who was doing the work in it. This is the real revolution in leadership in modern times.

Thanks to this standardization and organization, in combination with great technological advances and an almost inexhaustible source of energy (coal and oil), mankind was able to organize itself on a scale never previously seen. In the course of the last 100 years, the number of large organizations in many countries has grown exponentially. In Sweden in the year 1900, there was only one company with more than 2000 employees, a mining company. In 2015, there were 99 companies with more than 4000 employees.[36] In the same time, the population roughly only doubled, which means that the number of big companies in relation to the population size has increased tremendously. Since the start of the industrial revolution, at least, the trend seems to have been "bigger is better". Growth, both in financial terms and personnel is one of the top priorities for most companies. But why is that? Why is the natural tendency for organizations to grow larger?

Of course, gathering a lot of people in the same organization brings a lot of benefits. In management literature, the primary benefits are described as *economies of scale and scope*. Increasing the number of produced units leads to lower cost per unit, if done well, which means larger profit or at least survival in a market where prices keep going down through better utilization of resources, lower purchasing prices and knowledge accumulation. The more you produce of something, the cheaper each part becomes, aka The Experience Curve, mentioned earlier. This, by the way, seems to be the origin of the CFO belief that *any* area of business can cut costs by 5-10% without losing quality or decreasing scope every year. Big organizations can also afford to hire experts and give them a career path, and of course, a big organization can afford to pay its chief executives better salaries and incentives than most small organizations.

There are also other benefits of being big. Instead of following the leader, big organizations can define their market and political environment and gain advantages of having global, internal markets for capital. Everything from contributing money to presidential campaigns to influencing future common standards to fit their product portfolio strategies. It is harder to brush off a mail from the CEO of IBM than from some small local company, whether you are a supplier, customer or politician. Size gives oomph.

But the main driver for size, I think, is human nature. A talented employee that gets more and more responsibility will be naturally inclined to grow his/her fiefdom and at the same time retain control of quality. It is fully understandable and even commendable. I had the same idea when I became a manager for the first time: I believed I could achieve more, faster, of what was expected of me when I had a team to support me than I could working alone. As I became more successful, more things landed on my plate, which meant that I tried to get permission to hire new experts, to help me do my job better. The same dynamic plays out for a CEO. Growing the organization a bit more may help to expand market share which in turn means more revenue, profit and pats in the back from the shareholders.

Cyril Northcote Parkinson, the inventor of *Parkinson's law of triviality*, told the same story in a slightly more cynical way in his masterpiece *Parkinson's law, and other studies in administration* from 1957. Parkinson had looked at statistics from the British Admiralty between 1914 and 1954 and come to the conclusion that the number of administrative staff grew by 5.6% per year, while the number of ships and sailors that they were supposed to administrate declined significantly. From this he formulated his law that "work expands so as to fill the time available for its completion" and that the natural inclination of any bureaucratic organization is to grow. He explained this by two rules: (1) "An official wants to multiply subordinates, not rivals" and (2) "Officials make work for each other."[37] Everything I have seen of corporate life confirms his observations to be true in the private sector as well. Shoemakers make shoes. Bureaucrats create bureaucracy, hence the name.

It works - we (should) work less

So organizations grew and are growing, and are using the CFO Philosophy to build efficiency and output. With significant results. For all of mankind's history up until the industrial revolution, population and productivity growth was slow or non-existent, by today's standards. Today, politicians can lose their job for "only" reaching a few percent growth in their country's economy. From 1820 until 2008, the growth was a staggering 1143%, or approximately 6% per year measured as real GDP per capita.[38] In recent decades, as automation increases, there has been significant growth in productivity, even though it seems to have levelled out in the last decade. Figures from the US Bureau of Labor Statistics indicate that output per hour grew at least three times between 1947 and 2000.[39]

We have become ever better at taking tasks that were previously performed by many different people and making them more efficient or automating them, making our reliance on "humanpower" smaller. When the industrial revolution kicked off for real, 50% of the population were engaged in farming. Half the population worked to feed the other half.[40] Of the other half, 36% were blue collar workers, many of whom probably worked supplying the farming sector with tools and material. Only 10% had "white collar jobs", defined as "professional and technical, managerial, sales and clerical jobs". I would guess that this figure roughly equals the clergy and aristocracy, and that the proportion has been more or less the same throughout history, even though it is hard to find statistics on this further back. Ninety per cent worked with their hands, ten per cent with their brains. Today, that ratio is almost reversed, at least in the western world. In 2013 in the US, 1% of the total population worked in farming while a whopping 61% were white-collar workers.

Zooming out of the current situation and explanations that include fancy words like "digitalization" and "Industry 4.0", I think I can summarize the situation quite easily. Fewer people than ever have to work for our common day-to-day survival and that has led to a boom in "think-work". When the Egyptians, 4000 years ago, figured out more efficient techniques of farming, they could release a part of the population from field-work to "other" work. That is when they built the pyramids. The same has happened in our time, but on a much larger scale. Instead of pyramids, we have built Las Vegas, the Jumeira Palm island and the Internet.

Life expectancy at birth in 1850 was higher than ever before, but considerably lower than it is today. In 1850, not a single country in the world had a life expectancy at birth over 40 years. The main killer was something that we do not think too much about today: infections. In fact, infectious disease was the prime killer in the US in the year 1900, where it caused 53% of all deaths. In 2010, the figure was 3%. In 1926, the president of the United

States' son was playing tennis on the lawn of the White House. He got a blister on a toe that later became infected, killing him. A few decades before penicillin, nobody was safe from dying of infectious diseases, not even the president's son. Today, only two countries in the world have a life expectancy lower than 50 years and the average expected lifespan at birth has almost doubled.[41] Clearly, we have – as a species – managed to create something completely unheard of.

In the same time that we have grown our output by 6% per year, we have also increased the amount of energy we produce by approximately the same figure. Since we started using coal, and then oil, as an energy source, the GDP growth and energy consumption have gone hand-in-hand. One explanation that has been proposed is that as we become more efficient, we use more energy. Another conclusion is of course that we cannot have economic growth without having access to increasing amounts of energy.[42] And if that is the case, then the question is: how much have new management techniques had to do with the growth in efficiency and output? When I was very young I came to the conclusion – after long, careful consideration – that the wind blew because the trees swayed. If the trees stopped swaying, the wind would cease. What if our fixation with "management" in general and the CFO Philosophy in particular is a misguided interpretation of the world? What if they are costly distractions to getting the job done?

The world is changing again

Whatever the true merits are of the CFO philosophy, the current problem can at least be clearly stated. The CFO philosophy works great in a limited context: where the variables are known, measurable and the work is simple (and boring). Or another way of putting it: the perfect environment to replace humans with machines. In a limited factory setting, it is possible to predict and control input, risks and outcomes, and we have become better and better at that. But now, more of us are entering the world of the "unknown unknowns". In 2014, The Economist published an influential article called "Coming to an office near you: The effect of today's technology on tomorrow's jobs will be immense – and no country is ready for it". One of the central points of the article was that as much as 47% of today's jobs could be automated within two decades (based on a study from Oxford University). The writer then claimed that no country on earth is prepared for that sort of change. Educational systems, welfare systems and politic itself needs to undergo major changes to adapt to a future that demands less "humanpower".[43] The thing is, that future is already here. Fearing the future, we neglect to notice that it has already arrived.

Looking at the future from the past, I read John Maynard Keyne's *Economic Possibilities from our Grandchildren* from 1930. Writing at the beginning of the Great Recession, he gave the following projection: "In quite a few years-in our own lifetimes I mean-we may be able to perform all the operations of agriculture, mining, and manufacture with a quarter of the human effort to which we have been accustomed."[44] He was right, today 98% of farm jobs are gone in the western world. Those jobs have largely been replaced with jobs that require creativity, motivation and an ability to deal with uncertainty on a daily basis. Where we previously needed muscle and time, we now need hearts, minds and luck. Using the CFO Hammer ever more frequently will not solve the problems that come with this shift.

All work, no play

Even though we are more efficient than ever, we do not see that in a commensurate reduction in working hours. When I was a kid, my father came home for dinner with the family every day and my mom was a full-time homemaker. Only the very high earners seem to be able to afford a single income today, and few of my friends regularly make it home for dinner with their kids and spouses. A senior partner of a management consulting firm in the UK told me a few years after his firm was hit by the recession of 2008: "We have had to make some changes, we don't invest as much in team-building events any more, and we don't allow our staff as much free time as we used to." It probably came out different than he intended it, but the fact was that his firm was well known for pushing employees to do 80-hour work weeks even before the recession. His comment made me think that serfdom had reappeared, but this time it was "voluntary". As Foucault expressed it "A stupid despot may constrain his slaves with iron chains; but a true politician binds them even more strongly by the chain of their own ideas." [45]

This is not what our forefathers envisioned. In 1967, the American TV icon Walter Cronkite ran a documentary program on "The 21st century", talking about how life would be like for Americans in the year 2001. He cited a government report that concluded that Americans of the year 2000 would only work 30 hours per week. [46] Decades before that, in 1930, economist John Maynard Keynes, in his previously mentioned pamphlet *Economic Possibilities for our Grandchildren*, predicted that what he called the economic problem – the daily struggle for subsistence and survival – would be solved within a hundred years. He predicted that we would be able to work 15 hour weeks in three hour shifts, but he also worried what that would do to us:

To use the language of today –- must we not expect a general "nervous breakdown"? We already have a little experience of what I mean -a nervous breakdown of the sort which is already common enough in England and the United States amongst the wives of the well-to-do classes, unfortunate women, many of them, who have been deprived by their wealth of their traditional tasks and occupations – who cannot find it sufficiently amusing, when deprived of the spur of economic necessity, to cook and clean and mend, yet are quite unable to find anything more amusing.[47]

Keynes thought that we had two basic needs: one was for survival, food on the table, clothes, somewhere to live etc. The other need was the desire to impress our neighbors, and that need seems insatiable. Or as the economist Tim Jackson phrased it: "We spend money we don't have, on things we don't need, to make impressions that don't matter." So we work more and more, but doing what? Keynes thought that we would only need to work three hours a day and spend more time on culture instead. From a purely survivalist standpoint, he was probably right, but recent developments in working hours have rather gone in the opposite direction.

It is difficult to get an approximation of how much people have worked throughout history, including today. The first challenge is to define what is work and what is not. The distinction between work and free time is a modern invention. A smith, servant, farmer or aristocrat of the past worked when he or she needed or wanted to (depending on profession), not according to defined intervals on a clock. Some limiting factors existed, primarily light: before kerosene and electric light, the day usually ended when the sun set and the night was a place for drunkards, prostitutes and criminals. Physical presence in the workplace was important because communication technology was limited to traveling by horse or walking, which made "work-from-home" an impossibility, unless the home was the work. Blurring the lines between work and "free time" required physical presence. Lords lived in a castle on the land they governed. The parson was given a rectory in their parish. In the early days of the industrial revolution, the workers were provided with places to live on site where they worked, sometimes together with health care and other benefits that had the added effect of keeping people close to or on the job as much as possible.[48]

Today, technology voids the need of physical proximity to the workplace. When I first reached the higher echelons of a corporation, my boss told me "The company pretty much owns your time now." That is nothing new in senior positions, but in combination with smartphones, e-mail and social media, there is an added element of always being reachable and always being watched. In combination with what cartoonist Scott Adams (father of Dilbert) has termed "The Disruption economy", the effect is almost constant vigilance. Adams has made the case that Google, Apple, Samsung and others have business models that are built upon interrupting their users as often as possible with ads, commercials and notifications. "Individually, each company's interruptions are trivial. You can easily ignore them. But cumulatively, the interruptions from these and other companies can be crippling [...] I don't mean to sound like an alarmist, but I think this is the reason 80% of the adults I know are medicating."[49] Looking back at our time from 100 years in the future, I think there is at least a chance that when talking about "the Great Depression" we will mean the mental health problems of today's humans, not the fluctuations in the market.

As I approached the pinnacle of my corporate career, I was introduced to the concept of "staying power". When managers came to the really high positions in my company, staying power became one of the most important criteria for getting offered a position. Staying power, in my interpretation, means your ability to take heat. In top positions, skills are not enough. There will always be things that you cannot solve, or have not gotten around to yet, and you will get beat up for it. Competitors, market analysts, media, even your own staff will criticize you and someone will always be eager to take your place in the hierarchy. Staying power in that context, is basically a measurement of how much crap you can take before you lie down in a fetal position and cry. Pretty depressing, but not new.

So the question arises again: if we have increased our efficiency as much as Keynes predicted, why do we still work so much? I do not think the answer to that question is simple. It involves increasing expectations, more consumer products, globalization, and other factors, but control bureaucracy accounts for a lot of the working time in big organizations today, and it is both draining and counterproductive.

Whipping them into shape

Brand new in my management position, I decided to do what I thought good managers did: meet with the staff individually. I had some 20 staff, separated on three different functional units. As I sat down with one of the more colorful characters, John, I asked him which sub-unit he belonged to, as I had not been able to ascertain that from the paperwork. "Oh, don't bother looking for me in the systems," answered John, "as far as the system is concerned, I am a piece of test equipment." I looked it up and sure enough, he was right. Years of integration, "synergy-effects", cost-cutting, recruitment bans and trying to get rid of consultants had left us with a system that made it almost impossible to get our work done. In response, the employees got more and more creative in finding ways around the system. John, who was a real human, originally came into the company we both worked in as part of an acquisition long ago and had since then been registered as an expense for a piece of test equipment. My unit bore all the costs, but did not have to tangle with the HR department about trivialities such as pensions, vacations, evaluations etc. All that was handled by John's home unit (in another country) which simply charged his costs to the head office without being very transparent about what those costs were. And good luck it was for me, as John was exceptionally brilliant and hardworking, but somehow did not fit into the system. Somebody, somewhere, had met their quotas, but the quotas could not fit (or prevent) John's existence in the organization.

This story, I think, is typical of most large organizations.

When the CEO presents a bad report to the market, he or she promises strong measures, often cutting costs by reducing staff and getting rid of all the consultants.[50] Naturally, the organization is reluctant to do that if it will hurt their targets. Inevitably, there will be slow progress, or at least slower than the CEO has promised the market. Control functions are set up, usually run by the CFO and HR, and they will start generating control systems. The business, on the other side, will find ways to get the job done by circumventing the control functions. This game of cat-and-mouse has probably always existed, and the business usually gets what they want in the end as they have vastly more resources to think about this than the – often overburdened – control functions do. The net effect is that the system becomes more bureaucratic. My personal observation has been this: good people will always try to do the right thing, regardless of what the rules say. Bad people will always find a way around the rules. But the more you tighten your grip, the more slips through your fingers. Rules designed to stop a few rotten eggs from doing harm become a collective punishment for all the people trying every day to do the right things. As Henry Royce, of Rolls-Royce, is supposed to have said: "Every additional step in a process adds time and cost but not necessarily value."

Control through bureaucracy has always been used, but today's technology makes its reach wider than ever. The German software company SAP has introduced Enterprise Resource Management on a global scale and it or similar software can now be found in most larger organizations in the world. By connecting sales to logistics to production to finance, the Germans have made it possible for CFOs to have almost instant control over resources in the organization. Dashboards and Big Data combine to give companies like e-Bay and Amazon real time control over their operations. 4G and 5G Technology allows vehicle manufacturers like BMW and Scania to monitor their fleets continuously. But the systems, while getting better in most technical aspects, are no better in capturing human aspects. The accumulated effect, in fact, is that they are getting worse. For two reasons: the technological reach makes it tempting to try to control more and more things, and the majority of the types of jobs we have today require more of the hard-to-measure human elements: creativity, integrity, motivation and wisdom. SAP does not have a module for that. I will discuss some of the effects later in this chapter, but first, something so obvious that every executive should be forced to keep it on a note in their wallet at all times.

Goodhart's law

My friend Catherine had just completed her PhD when she started working for a major corporation, doing business-to-business sales. When she sat down with her new boss and went through her targets, the boss told her that she was expected to meet with each client on her client list at least seven times during the year. Being brand new to corporate life, Catherine accepted this without further questions, and started executing. Soon she discovered that the clients were reluctant to meet every other month. They asked Catherine why she wanted to meet so soon again, did she have any new products or data that they needed to know about? The answer was "no", it was still the same products, the main driver to meet was the internal goal of seven meetings. Catherine could see that she was behind target and grew ever more frustrated and insecure. The clients were annoyed by her insistence on new meetings. Finally, she opened up to one of her colleagues and asked her how she was able to get seven meetings per year in the calendar with each customer. The colleague responded: "Oh dear, nobody taught you how this works?" It turns out that all the other salespeople made sure to "run into" clients whenever possible. Instead of posting a letter, they took half a day out of the calendar to deliver it personally and hoped that along the way they would bump into some other clients. A nod from the client in their general direction in the hallway was counted as a meeting. Catherine could not believe it. The colleagues spent valuable time driving back and forth, stalking clients just so they could tick off their goal lists instead of working independently in the best way to improve relations with the customers.

The reason behind Catherine's company's implementation of the sales goal is the so-called "rule of seven touches". It is an old rule-of-thumb within the sales profession that you need to "touch" the customer seven times before you make a sale, through phone calls, meetings, web interaction etc. The reason is that it takes seven touches to build the intimacy and trust that is required to close the sale. Some organizations have taken this literally and made it a goal for their sales people. The problem is that when the meeting itself becomes a target you lose the "mojo" that made the seven touches useful in the first place. Instead of building confidence with the client, you annoy them by insisting on meetings with no real purpose other than fulfilling an internal target. When I was on the buyer side it was clear to me which companies employed this strategy and which did not. The ones who did were super-annoying.

The dynamics behind this inversion of results has been beautifully explained by Charles Goodhart. Goodhart was an academic and advisor to the Bank of England when he formulated what came to be known as "Goodhart's law", in 1975: "When a measure becomes a target, it ceases to be a good measure." The reason is that incentives, conscious and subconscious, appear that make people manipulate the results, especially if you make people's job security or bonus dependent on reaching the targets. The more unrealistic the target is, and the higher the pressure, the more manipulation will occur.

"Fuck the fucking numbers"

The most entertaining depiction I have seen of the numbers

game in fiction is the TV-show "The Wire", a police series set in Baltimore that follows groups involved in one way or another in the drug war of the city: the police, the gangs, the media, the politicians and normal citizens. An underlying theme to the whole series is what the show calls "juking the stats". The Baltimore Police Department is shaped politically by their need to meet vital crime statistics targets that have been promised by the politicians to the public. The message from the police leadership is clear: "I don't care how you do it, just fuckin' do it." Make the numbers. So the cops on the street arrest small-time criminals instead of chasing the big ones (which takes longer time). The police chiefs comb over the statistics and change "rape" to "assault" and "assault" to "simple assault". And nobody wins in the long run.

Late in the show, a new mayor is elected. An unlikely candidate, he has mostly watched the politics unfold from the sidelines and has made correct assumptions about the numbers game. "No more juking the stats," he promises the police officers in a meeting. But there is no easy solution. As soon as murder rates go up, the mayor's popularity goes down to the point where he is almost forced out of office. In a grim tradeoff between integrity and career, the mayor is forced to promise that he will make the murder rates go down again. And how does he do that? By pushing the police until they go back to their old habit of juking the stats. McNulty, the show's brilliant anti-hero, sums the situation up in words that would have made Shakespeare proud: "Fuck the fucking numbers already, the fucking numbers destroyed this department." In The Wire, everyone is a victim. The bad guy is the system. I quoted McNulty once to a salesperson who tried to sell me a dashboard. It did not go down well. But on the other hand, I did not buy his dashboard.

Everywhere, we see the effects of the CFO Philosophy being applied to ever more areas with ever more diligence. Teachers, doctors and police officers spend less time doing what they are supposed to do: teach, heal and protect, and more and more time filling in forms, writing reports and participating in internal meetings. And when the teachers, doctors or police officers complain to the politicians, the politicians – in the best case scenarios – promise more money for bureaucrats to manage the bureaucracy. But – as stated before – bureaucrats produce more bureaucracy.

In Sweden, "management by results" was introduced in the 1970s to increase efficiency and quality of public service. One of the measures introduced, with inspiration from private enterprise, was quantified goal setting. One may wonder how Sweden managed to become one of the richest countries in the world before the 70s without quantitative targets. What did they do before that? Professor Göran Sundström of Stockholm University has spent a large part of his career looking at the management by results in the Swedish public sector, and his conclusion is that it works much the same as it did before: the politicians influence the government agencies with three main instruments: 1) organizing the government agencies, including appointing key staff, 2) keeping tricky questions at arm's length and 3) through assessments and reviews. "Management by Results" has become an additional layer of bureaucracy that has very limited impact on the daily business.[51]

The public sector often looks – grudgingly – at its big brother: private enterprise, but to no avail. The corporations are leading the charge in becoming more bureaucratic. A 2011 study by Boston Consulting Group looked at the number of targets companies set themselves on top level. In 1955, "there were typically 4-7". In 2010, that number had increased – like so many other things – exponentially. By that time companies typically had between 30-60 targets on top level.[52] Who remembers that many targets? Apparently, no one.

Miller's law, named after George Miller, researcher at Princeton, states that the number of objects an average person can hold in working memory is about seven (plus or minus two), but when it comes to top level targets, the attention span is apparently even narrower. "Why strategy execution unravels and what to do about it" was published in Harvard Business Review in 2015.[53] The authors did an in-depth survey that was administered to 7,600 managers in 262 companies across 30 industries. Some interesting responses were found. For example, "More than 80% of managers say that their goals are limited in number, specific, and measurable and that they have the funds needed to achieve them." That sounds good. So even if corporations have more goals today than they used to, they are still clear and attainable, according to the managers. But wait. It turns out that "Only 55% of the middle managers we have surveyed can name even one of their company's top five priorities." Maybe those two things in combination answer the question why "[o]nly 9% of managers say they can rely on colleagues in other functions and units all the time, and just half say they can rely on them most of the time." So to summarize the situation: the managers are confident in their own abilities and they know their own goals, but they generally have a very vague idea of what the top goals of the company are and, as a result, poor understanding and knowledge of what their colleague's priorities are, outside of their own unit. Since the total number of goals are 30-60, that means that there is large potential for sub-optimization and conflicts of interest.

One example of that was given to me by a student at a lecture I gave to a course in change management. He told me that he had worked in the IT department at a private health care provider when the leadership team, urged on by the Corporate Social Responsibility director, decided that they were leaving too great a footprint on the environment and decided to reduce the total number of printouts by 50%. This generated lots of work for the IT people to devise new IT systems to replace the paper handling, but the work was halted halfway through the year when the legal department found out that the "print quota" imposed by the leadership team was too small. By law the corporation was required to keep certain archives on paper and it was not possible to do the paper saving and comply with the law simultaneously. Of course, somebody should have asked the legal department before they decided on the goal. And they should have had cross-function coordination meetings with the CSR team, IT and legal. And why not bring in Communications as well, and Security, because nobody likes to feel left out.

And that is just what happens. The Boston Consulting Group study found that middle managers in many organizations spend between 70-100% of their time in coordination meetings or writing different kinds of reports. This is analogous to my own experience. Or as a coworker that I overheard in the elevator one morning expressed it: "I haven't worked for 7 years, I just go to meetings."

Every support function I have ever worked with has used some variant of "we need to work closer to the business". One strong motive for doing this is of course not to be left out when important decisions are made. With a centralized, top-down, metric model that makes sense. The decisions are made in the leadership team and then supposed to be "executed" or "cascaded" in the organization. An effect of this is that the leadership teams are "ballooning" as everyone wants a seat at the power table. I have not found data to support it, but I am convinced that leadership teams have grown in size the last fifty years, along with the increase in numbers of targets. The result is a dreary environment where executives spend full days in meetings, listening to poorly structured PowerPoint presentations, while the real decisions are made elsewhere in small, informal groups or in the hallways.

Another effect of aggregating all the decisions to top management is that a bottleneck is created that is almost sure to make the wrong decisions most of the time. My experience in reporting to top-top management is that they are always asking for better quality of information, in the sense that they do not want 200-page documents to read. They want a condensed version that takes up 2-3 slides maximum. But when you try to condense information generated by hundreds or thousands of knowledge workers with highly developed skillsets in complex areas you need to make quite a few reductions. Again, that is easy if we are talking about problems with known and few variables (the McDonalds cash register, or shipping goods from Amazon), but most businesses today face "sticky problems" on a global scale.

When there are too many targets, employees start making their own priorities between them, based on what they perceive as most important at the moment. When priorities are made, things will be neglected. Case in point: Volkswagen. When the diesel exhaust manipulation scandal erupted in 2015, one of Volkswagen's mottos were "Sustainability and Responsibility". A few months before the scandal erupted, the company received the "2014 World Environment Center Gold Medal Award for Sustainable Development.[54] But clearly, despite talking the talk, Volkswagen deliberately cheated on emissions testing in the US. How could it happen? The leadership claimed that some rogue engineers took matters into their own hands. But really, what would be the point in doing that? Volkswagen had hundreds of goals, priorities, strategic focus areas et cetera, but the main one that was reiterated by the CEO Martin Winterkorn was that Volkswagen should be the number one car manufacturer in the world by 2018.[55] Maybe bad business decisions put Volkswagen in a position that they could not back out from, maybe it was just raw ambition, but I have a hard time believing that a whole group of employees would conspire to commit illegal actions for very little personal gain. My guess is that as the pressure grew and the target of being number one in the world was threatened, executives across the company started feeling the heat and sent explicit and inexplicit orders to the organization to "fix the problem, or else ... (but spare us the details)."

In 2016, a scandal erupted in Wells Fargo, a US bank. As a result of tough sales goals, employees at the bank had begun creating accounts for their customers, without informing them about it. Thousands of employees were fired and ultimately the CEO was forced to step down. The scandal continues, and in October 2017, the new CEO, Timothy Sloan, issued a Youtube video where he apologized to customers, shareholders and the public at large. The video is obviously scripted and reeks of corporate jargon, but the real coup-de-grace was given by reddit user u/arbiterxero in their summary of what Sloan had to say:

> "We fired some middle management who can take the blame for the ridiculous and unattainable goals we put in front of them.
>
> We told them to perform or lose their jobs and you'll be happy to know they lost their jobs anyways.
>
> [...]
>
> Thank you for trusting that we can find new scapegoats."

I do not believe that there was an evil genius somewhere inside British Petroleum that conspired to pump oil into the Mexican Gulf, or that a group of maniacally laughing engineers inside Volkswagen plotted to deceive American authorities. I believe that those disasters are logical effects of the CFO Philosophy and the CFO hammer hitting ever harder on organizations that were pressed already, and that we will see more of that as the world grows ever more complex, unless we rethink our basic assumptions about the world, how humans function and adjust our ways of leading to reflect it.

Out of control

Volkswagens "Dieselgate" is just one of many corporate scandals throughout history. Every time something happens, we wish that it would not have happened, and then try to make sure it will not happen again. The more control we *can* have, the more control we *want* to have. But it comes at a price. One price is increasing volume and complexity of legislation, which in itself makes control harder.

The collapse of WorldCom and Enron in 2001 led to stricter US regulation around financial reporting. The legislation, called the Sarbanes-Oxley Act, was introduced in 2002 and required all corporations that wished to be registered on the US Stock Exchange to comply to a complex set of rules. In a sense it was a unilateral, extraterritorial law. And since then, other countries have followed suit. South Africa has imposed its anti-corruption laws on foreign companies since 2008. The United Kingdom's Bribery Act went into effect in 2011 for all companies doing business in the UK. Mexico, Canada, India and Brazil have also developed their own laws with extraterritorial elements since 2001.[56] In 2016, the General Data Protection Regulation (GDPR) was adopted by the European Union, applicable to all companies that do business with EU citizens. And these examples are just a few examples of legislation that has hit public and private organizations in the last decades. Just like with targets, the idea that more is better is rarely opposed.

Or rather, many agree that we have too many laws, in general. But few of us are willing to remove laws, in particular. The opposition against each new law is generally weak. Typically, companies will grumble about inflexibility and cost increases. Individuals will make fiery speeches about integrity and privacy, but ultimately the arguments on the other side are often more emotional and convincing. It is about preventing the next terrorist attack. Or making sure our financial system stays intact. Or that workers are not suffocated in mines. Who can argue against that? Once the law is in effect, it is hard to remove it. Kip Hawley, who served as head of the Transportation

Security Administration between 2005-2009, has written about the problems he faced when trying to change the system.[57] Appointed by then President George W Bush in 2005 he set about to change a system that he believed was poorly adapted for its purposes: "In attempting to eliminate all risk from flying, we have made air travel an unending nightmare for U.S. passengers and visitors from overseas, while at the same time creating a security system that is brittle where it needs to be supple." He soon discovered that reason was not going to suffice in changing the system. He found out that politicians and the public were very reluctant to remove bans on things like lighters, knives and box-cutters even though the professionals agreed that allowing them to be brought on board would lead to minimal risk increase, while giving the screeners more time to look for serious threats. "Looking at the airport security system that we have today, each measure has a reason – and each one provides some security value. But taken together they tell the story of an agency that, while effective at stopping anticipated threats, is too reactive and always finds itself fighting the last war." But even though Hawley was the boss of the whole agency, appointed by the world's supposedly most powerful person – the President of the United States – he could not bring about any significant change during his tenure. The bureaucratic, political and public perception obstacles fettered him to his throne, as it were.

The draconian security checks that were introduced after 9/11 and gradually expanded since then may have mitigated some risks, but certainly created others. Take the prohibition against bringing liquids on board, for example. It makes it harder for terrorists to bring bombs on board the planes, but in reality, it just moves the risk from the airplanes to the waiting halls. I have often reflected on the fact that when I forget myself and bring a bottle all the way to the security check in, it is unceremoniously dumped in a trash can next to the line, without anyone registering my name. Say that I was a terrorist (I am not, I assure you) and I wanted to cause chaos and destruction, why not send ten friends through the check in, dumping one bottle of explosives each in the trash can, take a flight out and be safe and sound when the bomb erupts in what has now become the most densely packed area of any airport; the waiting line? Of course, you could add another routine, like registering the names of the passengers who dumped a bottle, having blast proof trash cans or x-raying every bottle that is dumped, but all this costs time and money, and there will always be other risks. For example, terrorists getting into the waiting hall, which happened in the Brussels terrorist attacks of 2016, when two terrorists set of bombs in the departure hall of Zaventem, Brussels airport. The next step is then to further restrict the departure and arrivals halls, but that will create queues outside the airport, and they in turn will be vulnerable to other attacks.

Before 9/11, cockpit doors were left unlocked and nobody considered it a problem. For almost 90 years of commercial aviation, there were no regulations mandating the door to be locked. There were some incidents, but nothing got enough attention to warrant stronger requirements. After 9/11, when the attackers gained entry to cockpits and flew their planes into the World Trade Center buildings and the Pentagon, many countries enacted laws that required advanced locking procedures to be installed on all commercial aircraft. The laws brought costs, of course, in the shape of installation investments, but also in more hassle for the aircraft crews. But it was not enough.

On the 25th of March, 2015, Andreas Lubitz killed himself in the French Alps. Lubitz had previously been treated for suicidal tendencies and his death was a tragic event, even had he decided to do it on his own. Unfortunately for the passengers of Germanwings flight 9525, he decided to do it by crashing the plane he was piloting, killing everyone else on board in the process. All 150 of them. From the flight recorder, recovered after the crash, investigators could piece together what had happened:

Lubitz's co-pilot had left the cockpit, probably for a toilet break. When he tried to get back in again, Lubitz had locked the door and set the autopilot to aim for the ground. The co-pilot was unable to gain entry for the ten minutes long descent and the plane crashed into the ground. In the last moments of the flight recording, Lubitz breathing can be heard, together with banging noises from the co-pilot trying to break into the cockpit, and the screams of passengers as they understand what is about to happen. The protective measure became a weapon for the killer.

Nevertheless, it seems hard for us to simply accept risk and not do anything about it. So we demand actions, which leads politicians to create laws, and then we do our best to comply.

Hard cases make bad law

The cost of compliance seems insignificant at first. There are already bureaucracies in place to produce the content matter, such as the political bodies and standards organizations. Maybe you have to hire an extra compliance officer or two. But every additional control layer adds cost and time, but not necessarily value. And the costs are absorbed somewhere in the system. Where? To an employee in a staff function of an international company, the costs become visible. Or rather, ubiquitous but invisible. IT engineers and finance people feel the pain in executing and signing off "controls", often without really knowing what they are for, other than the fact that they are Very Important. An industry has sprung up where software is being sold to "automate" control sign-off. But the problem, in most cases, is not the signing off itself, it is that the controls being signed off have little to do with the purpose of why they exist. Painfully sprung out of consultant-heavy analyses of standards and equally painful implementations in the organization they grow semi-obsolete quickly as the business evolves but the rules do not. Courtney's third law states that "There are no technical solutions to management problems, but there are management solutions to technical problems".[58] The IT systems usually serve to magnify management problems, not solve them.

Another hidden cost has to do with the attitude to ethics in themselves. As the compliance burden increases to the point that it almost suffocates the business, a sort of apathy spreads in the organization. The unspoken modus operandi becomes "anything that is not expressly forbidden is allowed". At that point, we have strayed away from the initial intentions of all legislation, which is, paraphrasing Hinduism and Buddhism: do no harm.

An investigation conducted by the British Cabinet Office in 2013 reviewed causes of complexity in laws. Richard Heaton, First Parliamentary Council, who commissioned the review states in the foreword: "[I]n my view, we should regard the current degree of difficulty with law as neither inevitable nor acceptable. We should be concerned about it for several reasons. Excessive complexity hinders economic activity, creating burdens for individuals, businesses and communities. It obstructs good government. It undermines the rule of law." Heaton states that "It is extremely difficult to estimate how much legislation is in force at any one time" but that the number and complexity of laws keeps expanding. As to why this is, Heaton offers the following explanation: "One of the key reasons for the increased volume of legislation may be that interest groups and individuals are becoming increasingly demanding of each other and expect the legislature to arbitrate on respective rights and duties, defining rules of engagement and setting boundaries to the unpredictability of life."

In 1842, Judge Robert Rolf made the following comment in the case of Winterbottom v Wright:

This is one of those unfortunate cases ... in which, it is, no doubt, a hardship upon the plaintiff to be without a remedy but by that consideration we ought not to be influenced. Hard cases, it has frequently been observed, are apt to introduce bad law.

The expectation that we can govern the interactions of man the same way that nature governs itself with the laws of physics, and that we can thus eliminate the risk and randomness in our lives is taking a large toll on our freedom, and not least free time.

Synthesis – More haste less speed

Ideas have consequences. If we think the world is predictable, controllable and that humans can be reduced to the same elementary input-output-mechanism as machines or physical objects, then that is the world we try to build. We construct all our models, IT tools, processes and management instruments on that premise, and since the premise is shared by almost everyone, any attempt to challenge it will be seen as obstruction. Try to suggest to any university educated, working person that you can run an organization without measurable targets and they will think you are crazy, or better yet, a hippie. Yet that is how organizations have been run since the dawn of time, and somehow humanity has managed to survive, and even thrive.

As we developed and embraced the CFO philosophy collectively, we let go of other things that do not fit as neatly in a "simple model", such as ethics, history, philosophy and much else that makes us human. When we are doing simple, repetitive things, those things are not very important. They can be governed from the top by laws, regulations, directives, KPIs and the other control mechanisms we have become so good at producing. But when the tasks are unpredictable, and the road is unknown, dependence on individual capabilities increases. It is elementary: if the tracks are laid it is easy to get to the end station. Any idiot with muscles can do that. But when the terrain is uncharted and the destination unknown, the captain must use brains to find the way, nerves to keep going and judgement to handle unforeseen obstacles on the way.

The world has changed. We are richer and more effective than ever before. Fewer and fewer of us have to work with our bodies. Instead we work with our brains. A larger part of the population than ever before are educated in both secondary education and universities. And when we enter the work market we are expected to be innovative, creative, take initiative and fulfil our destiny as "talents". But the machine ensemble is not created for that. It is created for control purposes and to root out the dependence on individuals. So we get unwanted side effects: bureaucracy, large scale mental illness, lack of innovation and random disasters.

During the great factory days, it must have been existentially challenging to pull the same lever in a machine two thousand times a day with no variation, but the difference between then and now was that at least the factory workers could see what came out of their work; a car, cloth, clothes or telephones. Going into almost any office today, it would be impossible to say exactly what is manufactured there. There input is done in front of one or several screens and the output is meetings (sometimes also used for input), paper and ... what else?

The best management literature today is not Harvard Business Review, Sloan Review or the Economist. It is Dilbert. Scott Adams manages to capture the essence of modern corporate life again and again, which can be seen from the sheer number of Dilbert strips that are displayed on doors and walls in offices around the world. What Scott Adams visualizes in his three-picture cartoons is the lack of common sense that pervades corporate life. Like a ritual that nobody really believes in, the interaction between the engineer Dilbert and his pointy-haired boss expresses an underlying existentialist crisis. It is reminiscent of the environment that the eastern Europeans captured in a joke during the Soviet era: "We pretend to work, they pretend to pay us."

I am not the first – by far – to have identified challenges in increasing bureaucracy. Everyone from McKinsey to Kafka have seen the problem, but maybe from different angles than my own. Some of them have even tried to provide solutions. And that is what the next chapter is about.

Chapter 4

New Trains on Old Tracks

"It's science, believe me"

Early evening, early autumn on an island in the Stockholm archipelago. A group of people between 30-60 years old sitting on yoga chairs in a large circle in a great room. The room is lit up by the most fantastic evening sun and there is a feeling, almost of reverie, in the room. The workshop leader smiles patiently, looks at each one of us, closes his eyes and says: "Can you feel the chemistry between us? It's in the air. It can be measured, it has been done. It is science, believe me!" The participants take turns to join the epiphany and heap praises over the group, each one more ecstatically euphotic than the previous. Until my turn comes up.

How did I end up here?

The seance was part of a course called "Living Well" that was held by volunteers from a non-profit foundation that aimed to better the world through "co-creation". I had landed here while searching for alternatives to the machine ensemble and could not believe what I was seeing. For all its "scientific" claims, the course was more spiritual than the church-led hallelujah meetings I had witnessed as an exchange student in Kansas in the 90s. The main difference seemed to be that the "religion" in this case was "science", laced with some Hindu and Buddhist concepts such as "compassion", "mindfulness" and "wisdom" and backed up by an endless playlist of TED talks. The participants were a curious mix of young world-savers, former McKinsey consultants searching for meaning and people from HR departments looking for ways to increase "motivation" in their workplaces. The purpose of the course was to teach the participants to find a better life through "evidence-based methods".

How to live a good life has been a topic for thought and discussion since the dawn of times, but this course did not bother with teaching Aristoteles, Zarathustra or Nietzsche. Instead it focused on newer "thinkers", mainly in the field of "spiral dynamics" that are well known in a small, continuously decreasing circle. Their claim was to have found faster methods of living better through science. Does it sound familiar?

Rationality, methods, evidence and evolution is mixed in a familiar compote but with a different purpose than the CFOs do it. The CFOs do it to make money, but these guys used the same methods and expected them to yield happiness, motivation, purpose and compassion. I found nothing of the sort and quickly abandoned that experiment, to the detriment of the workshop leaders. The rest of my weekend I was marooned on an island with people who saw me as an enemy to their salvation. They were just trying a new, simple method to save the world. How could anyone be skeptical to that?

The cycle of headless chickening

Management history is filled with examples of "silver bullets" that will fix the problems of today's business. Usually a new management trend begins with an article in Harvard Business Review with a bashful title like "The Strategy That Will Fix Health Care"[59], an idea spreads like wildfire in business press and management circles. Some executive somewhere, sweating over their 100-day plan, will bring in McKinsey or Boston Consulting Group and spend large sums on analysis, design and implementation. Eventually, it turns out that the ideas were not as revolutionary as first thought and the results refuse to validate the vision, but by then the executive will have moved on to other positions or disgrace. Another executive is appointed to "fix the problems" that the predecessor caused, and the cycle repeats. The only ones that make money from it are McKinsey and Boston

Consulting Group. Eventually, many of the consultants suffer some sort of mental trauma from experiencing the same thing over and over again, like a bad dream, and look for salvation outside the business press.

"Digitalization" is a current concept that will soon be replaced by something else, but the underlying story is old. There is a simple system to solve complex problems. Looking back at past management ideas, there is little reason to be cheerful. In the 90s it was ISO9001 and Total Quality Management that would save the day. Today management is not overly excited about their achievements. Then it was Six Sigma and Business Process Reengineering. Today, we implement Lean, Agile and Holocracy (for the slightly more brave/crazy). Articles that present 10-point lists for being a better boss/lover/employee abound. But none of them seem to do the trick.[60] So management throws them on the trash pile and move on to the next idea. But they do not die, they just take up residence somewhere in the organization, waiting for a new spring. Old ideas don't die, neither do they fade away, they reincarnate. Somewhere in the organization, there is an expert who was recruited or sent to an expensive training to become champion of something. Somewhere there is an executive who believed in them and sponsored them. In a large organization, a lot of them get great at surviving by paying lip service to whatever is the new management fad. Yesterday's TQM-champion is todays AI-driver. The motivation I can only guess, but it is probably a combination of habit, desire for job security and genuine zeal.

The problem is, if the new "tools" are built on the same assumptions as the old ones, then they will not solve the problems they created. Like replacing the old train with a new, faster one but keeping the tracks and then being surprised that the train ends up in the same destination again. As long as we create "holistic" systems based on the belief that the world is predictable, controllable and can be reduced to numbers, the results will be more or less the same.

Cultural anthropology 101

I am writing this paragraph at a lousy café in New York. As I look out at the streets to forget my sweaty $18 Croque Madam I see police cruisers passing by with three words printed on their doors: "Courtesy, Professionalism, Respect". Let me do a thought experiment: say my great-great-grandfather, Ola Henriksson, took the boat over from Europe to seek fortune in the New World, but through some fluke in time ended up in today's New York. No doubt many things would puzzle him greatly. The words written on the police cars would be one of those small mysteries that without an introduction to the present world would be very hard to understand and would maybe nag at the back of his mind while he dealt with the larger issue of surviving. Why are those things written on the cars? Is it an instruction to the police officers? Why are they then written on the outside of the cars where the officers cannot see them? Or is it a declaration of what is inside the cars (like in Ola's time they wrote "Beer" or "Blacksmith" on the outside of buildings or wagons to declare the inside contents). But then why is it not "investigate, solve, arrest" or something like that?

In the 1980s, as big mergers and globalization started to be common it became apparent that just telling the organization what to do was not enough. Sometimes things happened that were not in the plans, and a lot of the time things did not happen as they were supposed to. Academics such as Edgar Schein started talking about "corporate culture", saying that there was something "in the water" in big organizations that was hard to define, yet could determine the success or failure of an entire organization. The realization was best memorized in a quote attributed to Peter Drucker: "Culture eats strategy for breakfast." There is plenty of support for that notion in history. Homer describes vividly in the Iliad and the Odyssey how the tides of war turn as the heroes lose heart and spread fear among their own troops. Tolstoy, Hemingway and pretty much everyone who has ever participated in and written about war support the idea that a battle can be won or lost depending on the mood of the troops of the day. I think everyone who has worked for some years have experienced situations where the culture in a workplace allows people to accomplish miracles, but also situations where working with a certain team can feel like being stuck in a tar pit: no matter what you do to crawl out you feel the suck from the pit pulling you down again.

So far so good, but when CFOs decided that this was something that could affect the bottom line, they sunk their teeth into it. And they did it by using the CFO hammer. "We need to change our culture," they cried, and gave their HR-organizations orders to make it so. The HR organizations, thrilled that the CFO remembered that they existed, bared their teeth and went to work. In true reductionistic CFO-fashion they started dismantling "culture" into parts that could be neatly portioned out in the organizations. A culture is based on values, they concluded. That allowed them to tackle the problem one piece at a time. Now it was just a matter of deciding which values were most important and then replace the existing ones with those. Roll it out in a three year project, base rewards on completion, and the CFO Hammer is complete. After some years, as management fads do, the idea migrated to the public sector, resulting in the "Courtesy, Professionalism, Respect" we can now see painted on every cruiser in New York. Every government agency in the US (and most of the rest of the world) seems to have its own values. The problem is, there is no evidence that it works.

Trying to influence peoples' opinions is tricky business, as anyone who has ever watched an election closely knows. Despite the trillions spent in campaigns over the world every year, results can rarely be taken for granted. And that is just to influence people to cast votes on one particular day. Changing attitudes about life is much more difficult. Think of the money spent on – and the methods used – to inform us about the dangers of smoking, or the need to be more tolerant to other races, or to eat less sugar and fats. Even with insane amounts spent, it is still the work of decades to change people's attitudes in particular issues. The resources that the HR departments have at their disposal are minute in comparison. Besides, years of hard culture work could be undone in an instant. ENRON went from a respected household name to a reviled manifestation of corporate greed in a matter of weeks. I wonder what that did to the culture of the people working there. ENRONs values were, by the way: "Respect, Integrity, Communication and Excellence". According to Netflix, another organization that has worked a lot on its culture, these values "were chiseled in marble" in ENRON's main lobby.[61] Fat lot of good they did there.

Ok, if we for a moment assume that this whole culture thing actually works, let us look at what values the companies choose. In a study from 2015 that tries to describe the value of corporate culture, researchers L., Guiso, P., Sapienza, & L., Zingales, went through the web pages of 679 companies to see what their self-declared values are.[62] Here are the top nine:

1. Integrity
2. Teamwork
3. Innovation
4. Respect
5. Quality
6. Safety
7. Citizenship
8. Communication
9. Hard Work

The median number of values was five per company. That means that most companies have had to choose a limited set of these values, presumably so it will fit better on their corporate folders and marble entrances. I agree, nine values are just a bit too much. ENRON had three of them but Excellence is missing from the list. NYPD only hit one of the top nine but added "Courtesy" and "Professionalism" to the list.

The question is, why do you have one thing on the list but not another? I understand that the lists get filled after hours and days of executive retreats where a consultant "workshops" them through the process. But how can you argue for leaving any of the general-sounding ones off the list? Is "Citizenship" not important for the NYPD? Or Teamwork for ENRON? Really, they are all equally important once they have been broken against.

The idea to have values, like many others, probably came from Plato. In *The Republic*, he identified them as four (makes a great sign in marble): Prudence (or wisdom), Courage, Temperance (or self-control) and Justice. In Nicomachean Ethics, Aristoteles develops them further into an overarching concept of virtue ethics. I may sound like a grumpy Elmer Fudd, but I think that very little of substance has been added to the discussion of values in modern times, although surely some sign makers have had more business now than in the past. Values are one of those things the CFOs and HR departments will never really have control over, and most of the time, it is a waste of time to even try (at least outside the line organization).

A bottom-up revolution

I have seen plenty of organizations that have tried to implement "lean" or "agile" methodologies, without realizing that they are not just "tools" but philosophies. The Manifesto for Agile Software Development is very short. It states the following:

We are uncovering better ways of developing
software by doing it and helping others do it.
Through this work we have come to value:

> Individuals and interactions over processes and tools
> Working software over comprehensive documentation
> Customer collaboration over contract negotiation
> Responding to change over following a plan
> That is, while there is value in the items on
> the right, we value the items on the left more.[63]

The implication of these few lines is more revolutionary than it may seem at first. If you squint your eyes and read between the lines, the Manifesto is actually quite opposed to most of what the CFO Philosophy stands for. It implies that generalizations and detailed predictions are not needed (or even possible), that control is counter-productive in software development and that if left to their own devices, people will actually do their best and make right choices on their own. Pretty radical stuff. And yet, many executives have embraced it whole-heartedly, but – in my view – without really realizing or accepting the consequences. Usually what happens is that Lean and Agile are implemented in an organization that runs the full-scale CFO Philosophy. While the engineers and software developers are left to their own devices – seemingly – all the control functions are retained. The yearly budget cycle runs its course, Key Performance Indicators are set up and dashboards established so the managers can retain control and all spending needs to be approved in SAP. But that misses the point completely, and effects quickly materialize. The software developers complain that "only the tools" were implemented. Or as one engineer said at a meeting: "We work exactly the same way, except now we stand up and look at a whiteboard instead of sitting down and looking at PowerPoint slides in meetings." Managers complain that the organization "isn't mature enough to handle Lean/Agile" and are frustrated by the perceived lack of control. One manager expressed his frustration: "Lean is the same as any other methodology, except now the lazy programmers don't have deadlines."

Again, I am not saying that this is exactly how it plays out in all organizations, but I think the pathology is common enough. Sometimes there will be a strong manager that protects his or her people from the bureaucratic machine, but I guarantee that the pressure will always be there to reintroduce the CFO Hammer, because by and large, that is how we are trained to view the world.

Synthesis - New trains on old tracks

Looking for solutions to problems of our time, we turn again to science. Quantifying and standardizing "compassion", "leadership", "motivation", "innovation" or "culture" we follow the exact same recipe that has caused many of our problems: we look for an objective, systematic approach to diverse problems. The recipe generates "tools" such as personality tests, "situation-based leadership" or "three easy methods for being mindful". All of this is peddled as being "evidence-based", and thus – by implication – irrefutable. The simpler the idea, the easier it is to market, but the world is not letting itself be fooled by easy methods. The complexity of humans, and our inability to capture the complexity leads to oversimplifications that hide the true problems, because the true problems are not possible to generalize.

The daily task of a knowledge worker typically involves solving problems that are complex or require creativity. Great inventions do not come from units that follow the ISO process for "innovation". Great leaders are not always good at coaching. Students of change management are not necessarily suited for managing change.

Some people are motivated by a bigger purpose, others are motivated by greed, yet others by fear. Some managers get results by scaring their staff, some by telling them exactly what to do, others by sharing a vision and getting out of the way. Some managers are intelligent, some are stupid. Sometimes they get results using a certain method, other times they fail.

That is just the way the world is, and ever so many lists and tools will not change that. And worse than that: by having a "tool, method or process" for every contingency, we abdicate from making the tough calls. The higher up I worked in management, the more complicated the problems became that I had to deal with. Simpler questions were usually dealt with further down in my organization and the ones that reached me did so because there were no simple solutions. The problems that reached me were usually dilemmas. A choice between several bad options, usually with unclear consequences. But that is and always has been the task of management and leadership. And there will never be a tool for that.

So where do we look for solutions? Well, by now, the reader will have understood that I am not going to advocate a "new" tool or an "evidence-based" method that will solve all our problems. So if I cannot look to the future for solutions, there is only one option left.

Chapter 5

The Return of Common Sense

Vox clamantis in deserto

We need to replace progress with repetition. That would be a much healthier world. Think of the Renaissance. Renaissance means rebirth. What they did was to say: "Look at these Greeks. It's great! Look at all this stuff that has been stuffed in under barrels for 2,000 years. Fucking brilliant! Let's do it!" **How to Stop Living and Start Worrying: Conversations with Carl Cederström Simon Critchley and Carl Cederström**

As I left corporate, I dedicated – with considerable financial risk – all my energy to finding a solution to the question: "if the current system is so bad – then what is the alternative?".

I stand at the end of a long line of clever and brilliant people who have seen and described the problems with the CFO Philosophy better than me. Elton Mayo arguably started the Human Relations movement in the 1930s, followed by a second wave of – mostly – American scholars in the 1950s: McGregor, Maslow, Warren Bennis, Peter Drucker and in their wake practitioners such as Robert Townsend and Alfred P. Sloan. Also in the 1950s, Cyril Northcote Parkinson undressed the emperor in "Parkinson's law", Charles E. Lindblom deconstructed the view of a large organization as "rational" in *The Science of 'Muddling Through'* and the Japanese started showing the world that corporations could be run successfully without "business plans" or "strategies".

In my time, the heroes are people such as Daniel Kahneman, who pointed out the flaws in the theory of rational choice that underpins the macroeconomics our economies are constructed upon and Nassim Nicholas Taleb, who attacked how we view and calculate risk, among many other things. On social media, Daniel Pink, Richard Branson and Henry Mintzberg talk about valuing humans for being humans, not numbers. Scott Adams points out the absurdities of corporate life on a daily basis in his comic Dilbert.

And yet – in the words of Marlo Stansfield of The Wire – the game stays the game. Every effort to change large corporations or government agencies are swallowed by the Excel sheets. Parkinson's law, published in 1957, rings as true to me today as it probably did to my grandfather.

And constantly, the question is: what is the alternative?

After a year of looking, I still had not found the answer. Anything I spat out sounded like a motivational quote from LinkedIn. "Trust is important", or "Flatten the hierarchies". I could think of nothing that had not already been said a gazillion times by motivational speakers at conferences. The deeper I got into it, the more shallow it seemed. I slowly became aware of the awesome high-ground the CFO Philosophy occupies today: 1) it promises results through action and 2) anyone who wants to replace it needs to come up with something "better".

Current non-fiction literature, almost no matter what the topic is, tends to follow the "McKinsey Rethorical Model": Situation – Complication – Resolution. This is how most management consultants construct their final report powerpoints: first show a situation that the customer knows, then highlight the reason McKinsey were brought in (the Complication), and then deliver the verdict: the Solution. The reason they get paid the big bucks. Or as my swim-coach in Kansas used to express it: first you butter them up, then you slip 'em the meat. There is an expectation that there will be a solution to every other problem.

But like many complex issues, the solution is not one thing. It is many things. It is dependent on the situation, the context, the personalities of the people involved. The priorities at the time.

Instead of a system, we need to look at the world one problem at a time. Some problems can be solved in systems, but far from all. Sometimes the answer is trust. Sometimes the answer is KPIs and metrics. Sometimes the answer is to wait and see. Sometimes the answer is hiring someone with a long experience, sometimes you need fresh energy. Instead of just using the CFO hammer, we need to use lots of different tools, each suited to the problem we are trying to solve. Actually there is an expression that catches this: Common Sense.

The very basis of the global management consulting industry is a departure from common sense. Who in their right mind would hire someone 30 years their junior, just out from a business school, for outrageous sums of money to advise them on how to run the business they have been working in all their lives? Still, it happens every day, but the reason is that you do not buy a person's time, you buy a system, supposedly distilled from experience in many different organizations, and heavily dependent on the CFO Philosophy. You buy a belief that general laws governing the actions of humans can be distilled just like natural laws can be distilled from observing nature, and that learning those mysterious laws will allow you to improve your organization.

Forget that. Take what you have learned, learn more from those who are more experienced than you. Use what you know to evaluate new information and its usefulness in the context you operate. Bring back apprenticeships, village elders and secretaries. Read the classics. Kill KPIs that you are not 100% sure add value. Talk to people instead of looking at PPT:s. Live a little, love a little. I have described the situation and pointed out the complication. You, dear reader, will have to find the solutions. Good luck. I mean it.

Quo Vadis?

What did I want to do with this book? The whole time I have been writing it I have been plagued by self-doubt and whatever the opposite of hubris is called. But I have continued, because I wrote this book for myself. Not the 2019 version of Jacob, but the 2009 version. The one that suddenly came into a position of power and only saw that the emperor was naked. The one that thought he was crazy because what he considered common sense was alien to the vice presidents around him. And he did not have any arguments to convince others of the mistakes they were going to make. Like Cassandra of Troy, I saw that things were going to end badly, but could not get anyone to believe my warnings. I have written this book for me. I believe it to be laced with thoughts and inspiration that I have picked up from various sources since then, and I hope that it will help someone else in my position. Will it change anything? I am not sure, I think not, but maybe it will mean something to someone like me somewhere in the world. And that would be enough.

What is it I am trying to say? I am trying to convince the reader that the way we teach ourselves to manage is broken. That we are teaching a small extreme of what management is really about. We are so focused on manipulative tools and methods for controlling outcomes that we make our workplaces sad and oppressive distractions from actually doing what we have chosen as a profession. We live in a time where most people get to choose their careers and choose them based on heart. Motivation should not be a problem! But it is, because so many of us spend most of our time immersed in internal meetings, reporting structures and KPIs that actually add very little to the success of our endeavors, or to motivation, for that matter.

I believe that with a more generous application of common sense, supported by a slightly different philosophy of management, we could make our lives and workplaces more human. Does it guarantee success? Of course not, silly you for asking. But removing some of the unnecessary bureaucracy cannot really hurt.

Endnotes

1. Fitzgerald, F. Scott. *The Great Gatsby* (Kindle Locations 59-60). Kindle Edition.
2. Florén, Anders. "Disciplinering och konflikt: den sociala organiseringen av arbetet: Jäders bruk 1640-1750." (1987).
3. Formosus was found guilty but was later rehabilitated. In theory, not in health.
4. Someone who knows their history well may argue that it was only formalised in the *Qadragesimo Anno* in 1931, but I would then counter argue that it has been a *de facto* principle long before then. A global organization with no means of global communication did not choose to be decentralised, it had to be. It was only in the time of the telephone that the principle had to be explicitly pronounced.
5. Duffy, Eamon. *Saints and Sinners: A History of the Popes.* Fourth Edition.
6. Taylor, Frederick Winslow. *The Principles of Scientific Management.* Harper, 1914.
7. http://wwwc.aftonbladet.se/nyheter/9810/11/vegan.html (Accessed Nov 30 2018)
8. Tolstoy, Leo. *Anna Karenina* (Best Russian Classics Book 6, trans. Orest Vereisky, Louise Maude, and Aylmer Maude). Location 7,775
9. Gray, John. *Straw Dogs: Thoughts On Humans And Other Animals.* Location 1,332
10. Hayek, Friedrich A. "v.(1979): The Counter-Revolution of Science: Studies on the Abuse of Reason." *Auflage, Indianapolis* (1979).
11. Disclaimer: just because I defend these things at parties does not need that I support them. Sometimes I am just bored.
12. https://en.wikipedia.org/wiki/Myers%E2%80%93Briggs_

Type_Indicator, (Accessed Nov 11 2017)

13. http://www.businessinsider.com/8-habits-of-highly-effective-google-managers-2011-3?r=US&IR=T&IR=T, https://www.nytimes.com/2011/03/13/business/13hire. html?pagewanted=1&_r=1&ref=business&src=me

14. De Montaigne, Michel. *Michel de Montaigne: Selected Essays* (Dover Thrift Editions, trans.. William Carew Hazlitt, and Charles Cotton). Location 259

15. Stewart, Matthew. *The Management Myth: Debunking Modern Business Philosophy.* p. 303

16. They have, as Nassim Nicolas Taleb puts it: "skin in the game".

17. Taleb, Nassim Nicholas. *Antifragile: Things That Gain from Disorder,* (Incerto) location 5460

18. Arthur C Clarke: any sufficiently advanced technology is indistinguishable from magic

19. https://en.wikipedia.org/wiki/Printing_press, accessed October 29, 2018

20. Englund, Peter. *Ofredsår: om den svenska stormaktstiden och en man i dess mitt.* Atlantis, 1993.

21. Hackett Fischer, David. *The Great Wave* ; Stearns, Peter. *The Industrial Revolution in World History*

22. You know it is serious when academia borrows a German word

23. Schivelbusch, Wolfgang. *The Railway Journey: Trains and travel in the 19th century.* Urizen Books, 1979.

24. Before GMT "London time ran four minutes ahead of time in Reading, seven minutes and thirty seconds ahead of Cirencester time and fourteen minutes ahead of Bridgewater time." Ibid.

25. Taylor, Frederick Winslow. *Scientific management.* Routledge, 2004

26. Stewart, Matthew. *The Management Myth: Debunking Modern Business Philosophy*

27. McGregor, Douglas. *The Human Side of Enterprise.* Annotated Edition (Kindle Locations 4767-4776). McGraw-Hill Education. Kindle Edition.

28. https://www.nature.com/news/over-half-of-psychology-studies-fail-reproducibility-test-1.18248 (Accessed Nov 30, 2018)

29. Or rather "Each time cumulative volume doubles, value added costs (including administration, marketing, distribution, and manufacturing) fall by a constant percentage." (*The Economist Guide to Management Ideas and Gurus* by Tim Hindle)

30. If this example does not convince you, then consider the state of the London Underground, the conspicuous absence of manned missions to Mars, or the fact that we do not have a global standard for how power sockets should look.

31. Gray, John. *Straw Dogs: Thoughts On Humans And Other Animals.* Location 121

32. An American physician whom I met at a training pointed out a flaw in my argument; from a US standpoint new patients actually bring in more money, as they pay for it. But for the society as a whole, my argument holds up because the cost is picked up somewhere even if the patients do not pay for it themselves.

33. Deci, Edward L. "Intrinsic motivation. 1975." PlenumPress

34. http://www.urbandictionary.com/define.php?term=HR (Accessed 29 Oct 2018)

35. Or, as Robert Townsend called them: "an industrial police force that also sells insurance"

36. https://www.va.se/nyheter/2017/12/04/sveriges-storsta-foretag/ and Ronald Fagerfjäll: Svenska företagsledare under 100 år. SNS förlag 2008. ISBN 9789185695829.

37. Parkinson, Cyril Northcote, and Robert C. Osborn. *Parkinson's law, and other studies in administration.* Vol. 24. Boston: Houghton Mifflin, 1957.

38. https://ourworldindata.org/economic-growth (Accessed 29 Oct 2018)
39. http://groups.csail.mit.edu/mac/users/rauch/worktime/output_per_hour.pdf, (Accessed 29 Oct 2018)
40. http://www.npr.org/sections/money/2015/05/18/404991483/how-machines-destroy-and-create-jobs-in-4-graphs, (Accessed 29 Oct 2018)
41. https://ourworldindata.org/life-expectancy, (Accessed 29 Oct 2018)
42. Warr, Benjamin S., and Robert U. Ayres. "Evidence of causality between the quantity and quality of energy consumption and economic growth." Energy 35.4 (2010): 1688-1693.
43. Coming to an office near you: The effect of today's technology on tomorrow's jobs will be immense—and no country is ready for it, The Economist, Jan 18th 2014
44. Keynes, John Maynard. Economic possibilities for our grandchildren. In: Essays in persuasion. Palgrave Macmillan, London, 2010. p. 321-332.
45. Discipline and Punish: The Birth of the Prison Michel Foucault, p. 102
46. http://paleofuture.gizmodo.com/3d-tv-automated-cooking-and-robot-housemaids-walter-c-512622506 (accessed Nov 18 2016)
47. Keynes, John Maynard. Economic possibilities for our grandchildren. In: Essays in persuasion. Palgrave Macmillan, London, 2010. p. 321-332.
48. A similar trend can be seen today where companies like Google, Spotify and others try to provide full service for their employees. Sure, it's a great benefit, but it also gives you no excuses not to work 80-hour weeks.
49. http://blog.dilbert.com/post/123459399486/the-interruption-economy, (Accessed 29 Oct 2018)
50. Because cutting costs is within CEOs control, but sales and

innovation are not.

51. Sundström, Göran, and Rune Premfors. "Vem håller i rodret-30 år senare?." (2010): p.2

52. https://www.bcgperspectives.com/content/podcasts/strategic_planning_people_management_human_resources_morieux_yves_key_to_boosting_productivity/ (Accessed 29 Oct 2018)

53. https://hbr.org/2015/03/why-strategy-execution-unravelsand-what-to-do-about-it Accessed (29 Oct 2018)

54. http://3blmedia.com/News/Volkswagen-Group-Receive-2014-World-Environment-Center-Gold-Medal-Award-Sustainable-Development#sthash.12aqgXx6.dpuf (Accessed 29 Oct 2018)

55. https://www.cnbc.com/2015/03/12/volkswagen-makes-a-big-push-to-be-no-1.html (Accessed Nov 30, 2018)

56. https://www.gfmag.com/magazine/may-2015/unavoidable-costs-increasing-regulation-compliance-goes-global, (Accessed Nov 30, 2018)

57. http://www.wsj.com/articles/SB10001424052702303815404577335783535660546 (Accessed Nov 15, 2016)

58. http://zvon.org/comp/r/ref-Security_Glossary.html#Terms~Courtney%27s_laws (Accessed Nov 14, 2018)

59. Porter, Michael E., and Thomas H. Lee. "The strategy that will fix health care." Harv Bus Rev 91.12 (2013): 24.

60. One hint could be this: if all your competitors implement the same model, then maybe it won't give you the edge you are hoping for.

61. https://jobs.netflix.com/culture, (Accessed Nov 30, 2018)

62. http://economics.mit.edu/files/9721 (Accessed Nov 30, 2018)

63. http://agilemanifesto.org/ (Accessed Jan 1 2017

BUSINESS
BOOKS

Business Books

Business Books publishes practical guides
and insightful non-fiction for beginners and professionals.
Covering aspects from management skills, leadership and
organizational change to positive work environments, career
coaching and self-care for managers, our books are a valuable
addition to those working in the world of business.

15 Ways to Own Your Future
Take Control of Your Destiny in Business and in Life
Michael Khouri
A 15-point blueprint for creating better collaboration, enjoyment,
and success in business and in life.
Paperback: 978-1-78535-300-0 ebook: 978-1-78535-301-7

The Common Excuses of the Comfortable Compromiser
Understanding Why People Oppose Your Great Idea
Matt Crossman
Comfortable compromisers block the way of anyone trying to
change anything. This is your guide to their common excuses.
Paperback: 978-1-78099-595-3 ebook: 978-1-78099-596-0

The Failing Logic of Money
Duane Mullin
Money is wasteful and cruel, causes war, crime and dysfunctional feudalism. Humankind needs happiness, peace and abundance. So banish money and use technology and knowledge to rid the world of war, crime and poverty.
Paperback: 978-1-84694-259-4 ebook: 978-1-84694-888-6

Mastering the Mommy Track
Juggling Career and Kids in Uncertain Times
Erin Flynn Jay
Mastering the Mommy Track tells the stories of everyday working mothers, the challenges they have faced, and lessons learned.
Paperback: 978-1-78099-123-8 ebook: 978-1-78099-124-5

Modern Day Selling
Unlocking Your Hidden Potential
Brian Barfield
Learn how to reconnect sales associates with customers and unlock hidden sales potential.
Paperback: 978-1-78099-457-4 ebook: 978-1-78099-458-1

The Most Creative, Escape the Ordinary, Excel at Public Speaking Book Ever
All The Help You Will Ever Need in Giving a Speech
Philip Theibert
The 'everything you need to give an outstanding speech' book, complete with original material written by a professional speech-writer.
Paperback: 978-1-78099-672-1 ebook: 978-1-78099-673-8

On Business And For Pleasure
A Self-Study Workbook for Advanced Business English
Michael Berman
This workbook includes enjoyable challenges and has been designed to help students with the English they need for work.
Paperback: 978-1-84694-304-1

Small Change, Big Deal
Money as if People Mattered
Jennifer Kavanagh
Money is about relationships: between individuals and between communities. Small is still beautiful, as peer lending model, micro-credit, shows.
Paperback: 978-1-78099-313-3 ebook: 978-1-78099-314-0

Readers of ebooks can buy or view any of these bestsellers by clicking on the live link in the title. Most titles are published in paperback and as an ebook. Paperbacks are available in traditional bookshops. Both print and ebook formats are available online.
Find more titles and sign up to our readers' newsletter at
http://www.jhpbusiness-books.com/
Facebook: https://www.facebook.com/JHPNonFiction/
Twitter: @JHPNonFiction